ACKNOWLEDGMENTS:

Special thanks to Madeleine Morel, Joann Davis, Howard Tharsing, Barbara Lowenstein, Grace Sullivan, Terry Wolf and Mark Camin.

YOU <u>CAN</u>

MAKE

A DIFFERENCE!

The nineties may well be the make-or-break decade in the fight for gay and lesbian civil rights—and this book provides a sensible battle plan for achieving equality. Grounded in well-researched fact, it will show you how to:

- ❏ resolve internalized homophobia—and move on

- ❏ evaluate institutional homophobia in businesses and organizations—and do something about it

- ❏ influence politicians—and deconstruct harmful popular myths

- ❏ successfully cope with gay-related family crises, whether you are a gay son or lesbian daughter— or the parent of a gay or lesbian child

- ❏ discuss homophobia with heterosexuals— calmly and constructively

- ❏ come out of the closet—and help others to do the same

- ❏ effectively fight homophobia in all walks of life.

HOW TO MAKE THE WORLD
A BETTER PLACE
FOR GAYS AND LESBIANS
will spur you into action—
and give you everything you need to fight
the good fight!

HOW TO MAKE THE WORLD A BETTER PLACE FOR GAYS AND LESBIANS

UNA FAHY

WARNER BOOKS

A Time Warner Company

Information regarding companies mentioned in this book was accurate as of January 1995.

Warner Books, Inc., 1271 Avenue of the Americas, New York, NY 10020

Ⓦ A Time Warner Company

Printed in the United States of America
First Printing: June 1995
10 9 8 7 6 5 4 3 2 1

Library of Congress Cataloging-in-Publication Data

Fahy, Una.
    How to make the world a better place for gays and
  lesbians / Una Fahy.
      p.   cm.
    ISBN 0-446-67041-3
    1. Homophobia—United States—Moral and ethical
    aspects. 2. Homosexuality—United States—Moral and
  ethical aspects. 3. Gay liberation movement—United States.
    I. Title.
HQ76.3.U5F328   1995
305.9'0664—dc20   94-42254
                                                                CIP

Cover design by Susan Newman

Book design by H. Roberts

Table of Contents

Introduction

I grew up in a sheltered, religious environment in which everyone assumed that when children became adults they marry a member of the opposite gender and have children. No one ever discussed homosexuality. As a result, I was fifteen before I learned from a classmate that there were gay and lesbian people in the world. She said that homosexuals were awful and if I was unlucky enough to encounter one I should run. I was eighteen before I had the dreaded encounter, and the lesbian I came face to face with was myself. It was the first time I consciously understood that the reason I had no interest in boys except as friends, was fascinated by the female form, and had a serious crush on a certain young woman was because I was a lesbian. My sexual orientation felt completely natural to me.

The first person I came out to was a teacher whom I respected. She was shocked and advised me to start dating boys immediately, behave like a lady, and always wear feminine clothes. Over the next few months I experienced a major dose of reality and grew up quickly. When I came out to friends most of them distanced themselves from me and my family did not want to deal with it. The world I had known was no longer a friendly or safe place for me to be. At this point in my life I only felt comfortable and happy in the company of other gays and lesbians, and even then I would meet homosexuals who hated themselves for being gay and this disturbed me more than anything. Later, I learned that this self-hatred was one example of what is called *internalized homophobia*. I realized that the negative things I had heard about gays and lesbians were wrong. We were not awful people but victims of a great injustice.

At that time (the late 1970s), I became involved in the gay and lesbian rights movement. Throughout the 1970s the movement gained incredible momentum. Many gay men and lesbians felt an immense excitement about how things were beginning to change. In large numbers, gays throughout the United States were rejecting the stigma society places on homosexuality and lesbianism, coming out of the closet, attending demonstrations, challenging homophobia, and working to obtain their civil rights. The result of these efforts can be seen today. Gay and lesbian rights issues are in the forefront of the national and local political scenes. Eight states have enacted comprehensive gay rights laws, while many local municipalities ban discrimination based on sexual orientation and extend medical benefits to domestic partners of gay and lesbian municipal employees. The business community is also responding to gay and lesbian visibility. A substantial number of corporations include sexual orientation in their nondiscrimination policies and a small but growing number offer benefits for domestic partners.

While it is important to acknowledge and celebrate the achievements, we must keep in mind that we still have a long way to go and much work to do before gays and lesbians attain full civil rights. When reading *How to Make the World a Better Place for Gays and Lesbians* you will learn the battle against homophobia must be fought on many fronts. On the political front, where the focus is on civil rights legislation and laws protecting gays and lesbians from hate crimes, I encourage the use of voting power and letter-writing campaigns to influence politicians, and emphasize the need to support and become involved with gay and lesbian political organizations. In addition, I devote a section to those messengers of hate and promoters of intolerance, the religious right. The backlash orchestrated by the antigay and lesbian forces of the religious right is one of the main challenges we face. By manipulating the homophobic feelings of the majority the religious right tries to convince voters to rescind gay and lesbian rights legislation and prevent new laws from being enacted. I provide a list of the organizations that belong to the religious right and suggestions for combating their unholy crusade against gays and lesbians.

On the personal front, I stress the importance of coming out, as well as dealing with internalized homophobia. Ultimately, the battle against internalized homophobia is the most important one to win. The greatest victory for homophobia is when gays and lesbians accept the negative views put forth by a homophobic society, resulting in the destruction of their self-esteem and their preventing themselves from achieving their full potential as human beings. It is for this reason that the gay and lesbian rights movement uses the word *pride* as a rallying cry.

Recognizing how important it is for all citizens to have full civil rights, many heterosexuals have become involved in the gay and lesbian movement. Other heterosexuals who view this movement as someone else's battle should realize that preventing gays and lesbians from obtaining their rights is just the first item on the agenda of the religious right. Their ultimate goal is to force the government to legislating their version of morality and to dissolve the separation between church and state. If they succeed—and they have had some success—everyone's rights will be in danger. For this reason I recommend that heterosexuals also become involved in this struggle, and many of the actions outlined in the book can be taken by both heterosexuals and gays and lesbians.

Within these pages you will find everything you need to combat homophobia, but it is up to you to become aware, get involved, speak up, and take action. Undoubtedly, on the path to a nonhomophobic society we will encounter barriers, and in order to achieve our goal of ensuring the dignity and civil rights of gays and lesbians we must combine education with action, be optimistic, and stay proud.

NOTE: The majority of the sections in this book are geared to all readers, gay and straight. Sections 3, 8, and 16, however, are directed toward gays and lesbians; sections 4 and 9 are directed toward heterosexuals.

HOW TO MAKE THE WORLD A BETTER PLACE FOR GAYS AND LESBIANS

1
Understand Homophobia

ho.mo.pho.bi.a *n*. an irrational, and persistent fear, dread, hatred of homosexuals or homosexuality.

BACKGROUND

I believe that gay men and lesbians are the most hated and feared people in America. While hatred of gays and lesbians has always existed in Judeo-Christian society, the recent rise of Christian fundamentalism has spawned numerous organizations that aggressively encourage Americans to reject progressive social change and return to the restrictions and hypocrisy of the past. Knowing that the majority of people are inclined to blame others for their own shortcomings, fundamentalists and some conservatives have convinced many Americans that gays and lesbians are responsible for the decline of so-called family values. Tolerance of homosexuality, they claim, is leading America down a path to destruction. This scapegoating, combined with the new gay and lesbian visibility, has caused gays and lesbians to become easy targets of hate crimes. An overwhelming majority have experienced some form of victimization based on their sexual orientation. This victimization ranges from name-calling, ridiculing, joke telling, to various forms of discrimination, exclusion from the mainstream, to extreme acts of violence. Despite the prevalence of this bigotry many people do not have a clear understanding of homophobia and its manifestations, nor do they want to dwell on this unpleasant issue. Yet if we wish to end discrimination and increase tolerance, we must face homophobia, identify it, and do something about it.

In a pamphlet produced by the Campaign to End Homophobia, Cooper Thompson and Barbara Zoloth present a comprehensive definition of homophobia. They classify it into four distinct but interrelated categories: personal, interpersonal, institutional, and cultural.

Personal homophobia is prejudice based on a personal belief that lesbian, gay, and bisexual people are sinful, immoral, sick, inferior to heterosexuals, or incomplete women and men.

Interpersonal homophobia is individual behavior based on personal homophobia. This hatred or dislike may be expressed by name-calling, telling "jokes," verbal and physical harassment, and other individual acts of discrimination.

Institutional homophobia refers to the many ways in which government, business, churches, and other institutions and organizations discriminate against people on the basis of sexual orientation. Institutional homophobia is also called **heterosexism.**

Cultural homophobia refers to social standards and norms that dictate that being heterosexual is better or more moral than being lesbian, gay, or bisexual, and that everyone is or should be heterosexual. Cultural homophobia is also called **heterosexism.**

Personal homophobia is a blanket term for homophobic beliefs and feelings experienced by gays, lesbians, bisexuals, and heterosexuals. Because the impact of personal homophobia on gays and lesbians differs in many ways from its impact on heterosexuals, I deal with both groups separately. Therefore, in order to avoid confusion with terminology when I discuss *personal homophobia*, I will be referring *only* to homophobic beliefs and feelings practiced by heterosexuals. When I discuss *internalized homophobia*, I will be referring *only* to homophobic beliefs and feelings practiced by gay men, lesbians, and bisexuals.

Homophobia exists in varying degrees. It can be subtle, overt, or extreme. To illustrate the different manifestations of homophobia I have compiled the following lists:

Examples of Subtle Homophobia

• Believing that gays and lesbians want special treatment. This is another strategy being used by politicians and organizations opposed to gay and lesbian rights. They maintain that gays and lesbians have the same rights as heterosexuals and are pushing for "special rights." The results of the November 1993 elections indicated that the majority of voters believe this propaganda. Antigay and lesbian rights initiatives were passed in Cincinnati, OH, Austin, TX, Lewiston, ME, and Portsmouth, NH, and the residents of four rural counties in Oregon (Douglas, Linn, Klamath, and Josephine) overwhelmingly approved measures that judged homosexuality to be "abnormal and perverse" and legalized discrimination against gays and lesbians.

• Using the expression "blatant homosexual." Have you ever heard anyone use the expression "blatant heterosexual"?

• Asking questions like "Why do they have to flaunt it?" Anyone, whether gay or straight, who asks a question like this is homophobic. What they are really saying is "Why do you have to be the way you are?"

• When a gay man or lesbian hides their gay magazines from heterosexual visitors. This is another sign of internalized homophobia and it demonstrates that these people are embarrassed by or ashamed of their sexual orientation.

Examples of Overt Homophobia

• AIDS disinformation. At this stage of the AIDS epidemic, medical scientists have enough data to determine the methods of contracting the HIV virus: sexual transmission, IV drug use, fetal transmission, and transfusions of infected blood. Homophobes tend to ignore this fact and use their so-called fear of contracting HIV to justify bigotry. For example, during the gays-in-the-military debate some soldiers rationalized their support of the ban by claiming that sharing living quarters with gay men would expose them to HIV infection. Then there is the well-publicized case of Rev. Ruben Diaz, a member of the New York City Police Civilian Complaint Review Board, who spoke out against the Gay Games on the grounds that the gays and lesbians participating in the event would spread AIDS in the city.

• Telling demeaning jokes. All oppressed groups are victimized by this type of "humor."

• Imitating an effeminate man (the limp wrist routine). I often see this stereotype on television. Ignorant people rely on stereotypes to reinforce their false beliefs. Shallow and inept comedians routinely exploit this image.

• Believing that lesbians are man haters. Most lesbians I've encountered never express strong negative feelings toward men as a group. Lesbianism is not about hating men; it's about women loving women.

• Undercounting the size of the gay and lesbian population. The more gays and lesbians there are the bigger the threat to the homophobes, and in order to ease their fears they routinely undercount the size of the gay and lesbian population. Antigay and lesbian rights groups rely on the findings of the Guttmacher survey (1993), which maintains that only 1 percent of the male population is gay. Homophobes fail to mention that this survey has major flaws, that 30 percent of the men asked to participate refused, and that the survey took no measures to deal with the fact that gays and lesbians tend to hide their sexual orientation. The Kinsey survey (1949 and 1954) found 10 percent of the population to be gay and lesbian. The Harvard study (1994) found that 20 percent of adults have homosexual impulses, and that 6.2 percent of men and 3.3 percent of women confirmed that they engaged in homosexual behavior in the past five years. Considering this, it is justifiable to estimate that approximately 10 percent of the population is gay and lesbian. Therefore, there are close to 25 million gays and lesbians in the United States. This is equal to the populations of Denmark, Ireland, Finland, and Greece combined.

• Using self-deprecating expressions when referring to one's sexual orientation. Gays and lesbians suffering from a bad case of internalized homophobia often try to gain approval from straights by ridiculing themselves and other homosexuals.

Examples of Extreme Homophobia

• All types of gay and lesbian bashing, including violence and intimidation.

• Believing lesbians and gays should be exterminated. Some extremist groups such as the Klan, neo-Nazis, and Skinheads advocate the extermination of homosexuals (see *Quarantines and Death: The Far Right's Homophobic Agenda* by Mab Segrest and Leonard Zeskind, published by The Center for Democratic Renewal). You should be aware that it could happen. Did you know that a quarter of a million gays and lesbians were murdered by the Nazis?

• Working for antigay legislation. Discrimination in any form is wrong. State-sanctioned discrimination is extremely dangerous and diminishes the integrity of the state.

• Denying housing to a person because of their sexual orientation.

• Denying employment to a person because of their sexual orientation.

• Disowning a lesbian or gay teenager. Families often disown their homosexual children, causing some teenagers to drop out of school, become homeless, be lured into prostitution, or become criminals.

• Committing suicide because of sexual identity. This is an extreme form of internalized homophobia and unfortunately still happens today, especially among teenagers.

Things to Do

• Be aware that homophobia affects different people in different ways.

• Be on the alert for subtle homophobia. Subtle homophobia is insidious because it is often difficult to detect, but it is as harmful as overt homophobia and must always be challenged.

• Look beneath the surface and learn the hidden language of homophobia; for example, people who champion "family values" may be using family values to disguise their homophobia.

• Don't mourn; fight. While it is natural for victims to feel victimized, we must be careful not to allow a victim mentality to dominate our lives. Stay optimistic!

• Contact the Campaign to End Homophobia and request pamphlets and other resources dealing with homophobia. Also, contribute financially to this organization.

• Read a comprehensive study of homophobia.

RESOURCES

Campaign to End Homophobia
P.O. Box 819
Cambridge, MA 02139
617-868-8280

Blumenfeld, Warren J., ed. *Homophobia: How We All Pay the Price*. Boston: Beacon Press, 1992.

Boswell, John. *Christianity, Social Tolerance, and Homosexuality*. Chicago: University of Chicago Press, 1980.

DeCecco, John, ed. *Homophobia in American Society: Bashers, Baiters and Bigots*. New York: Harrington Park Press, 1985.

Weinberg, Dr. George. *Society and the Healthy Homosexual*. Boston: Alyson, 1991.

2
Admit to Your Own Homophobia

BACKGROUND

Everyone, whether gay or nongay, practices personal or internalized homophobia on some level. The level can range from a mild uneasiness with homosexuality and lesbianism to outright hatred of all homosexuals. While it is vital for everyone to combat homophobia in the external world, it is also necessary to fight against our own homophobic beliefs. We must approach this struggle with a relentless dedication, keeping in mind that how we feel within ourselves will in many ways have an impact on the external world.

Our first step in combating personal or internalized homophobia is to admit that we indulge in it. Many progressive people, especially lesbians and gay men, are ashamed of their own homophobia and therefore they refuse to acknowledge these destructive feelings. Unless, however, we admit to our true feelings, no matter how mild they may be, we cannot effectively overcome homophobia of any kind and place ourselves in danger of being called hypocrites. Also, some individuals, gay and straight, honestly believe that they have overcome their discomfort with homosexuality or that they never felt it. These people have not looked closely enough at their own behavior, feelings, and thoughts. Subtle feelings or seemingly innocuous behavior often demonstrates degrees of personal or internalized homophobia. For example, you have a problem if you are uncomfortable in the company of an effeminate man or assume that everyone knows you are gay or lesbian even though you hide or never discuss your relationships with heterosexuals. If you think that you are in this category, then test yourself by answering the following questions:

1. Do you automatically think that effeminate men are gay? ___ yes ___no

2. Do you believe that many lesbians are man haters? ___ yes ___no

3. Do you associate gay men with promiscuity? ___ yes ___no

4. During a discussion that involved a homosexual, did you unnecessarily mention the person's sexual orientation? ___ yes ___no

5. Have you ever told a joke about a gay or lesbian? ___ yes ___no

6. Do you ever hide your sexuality when it is unnecessary to do so? ___ yes ___no

7. Are butch women lesbians? ___ yes ___no

8. Have you ever criticized a homosexual for "flaunting it"? ___ yes ___no

9. Does it bother you that 10 percent of the population is gay and lesbian? ___ yes ___no

10. Are you tired of hearing about gay and lesbian issues in the media? ___ yes ___no

If you answered "yes" to any of these questions, then you indulge in personal homophobia. This is not earth-shattering and you should not lament or feel bad about yourself. What you need to do is admit to the problem and take action.

Things to Do

GAYS

• List examples of your experience with internalized homophobia. Consider such issues as shame, guilt, self-hatred, stereotyping, closeting, and hostility toward other gays and lesbians.

• Reviewing each item on the list, ask yourself *why* you had this feeling or took this action.

• If you have difficulty understanding why you had a particular homophobic feeling or action, discuss it with a therapist (gay or gay friendly, of course) or participate in a workshop dealing with internalized homophobia. Counseling centers for gays and lesbians offer these workshops (see pages 15–16) or gay and lesbian groups in your community often have rap sessions. You can suggest that one of these sessions focus on internalized homophobia. Also, gay and lesbian youth organizations (see pages 15–16) deal with this issue.

• Learn the source of your homophobia. For example, after discovering that you were gay or lesbian, did your parents disapprove and attempt to change your sexual orientation? Were you ridiculed and shunned in school? Were you exposed to antigay and lesbian sermons in church or negative stereotypes in the media? Internalized homophobia manifests when we believe society's negative views of us. It is a vital part of the scheme to keep gays and lesbians oppressed. Knowing the source of our internalized homophobia is an important step to eliminating it.

NONGAYS

• List examples of your experience with personal homophobia. Consider the following issues: stereotyping, fear of the unknown, fear of diversity, resentments, discrimination, name-calling, and bashing.

• Be totally honest with yourself and examine each item, asking yourself *why* you felt that way or took that action.

• Learn the source of your homophobia. From whom did you learn your negative views of gays and lesbians? A parent, a teacher, a religious leader?

• Discuss your efforts with others.

RESOURCES

Blumenfeld, Warren, and Diane Raymond. *Looking at Gay and Lesbian Life*. Boston: Beacon Press, 1988.

Pharr, Suzanne. *Homophobia: A Weapon of Sexism*. Little Rock, AR: Chardon Press, 1988.

3
Learn How Internalized Homophobia Is Harmful

No one can make you feel inferior without your consent.

—ELEANOR ROOSEVELT

BACKGROUND

Throughout the centuries the heterosexual majority, using their concept of morality as a justification, has instilled society with the belief that homosexuality is abnormal and an affront to God, that gays and lesbians are sick and perverted, and that their sexual orientation should not be tolerated. These irrational and prejudicial teachings have had a negative effect on everyone, gays and lesbians in particular.

Gays and lesbians often internalize society's negative views of their sexuality, denouncing themselves and weakening their self-esteem. After all, when children are programmed to believe that the norm is heterosexual, that deviation from the norm is wrong and will be punished, it is easy to understand why some gays and lesbians ask themselves, "Am I acceptable?" It is difficult therefore for gays and lesbians to maintain healthy self-esteem when confronted with the destructive attitude of society. The degree to which gays and lesbians experience internalized homophobia varies from mild to extreme. Whatever the degree gays and lesbians must understand that internalized homophobia has a profound, negative effect on their psyche. While they must continue to teach heterosexuals the truth about homosexuality, they must also work on their own homophobic beliefs. This struggle requires an honest, fearless, and thorough exploration of their inner world.

Fortunately, in recent years many gays and lesbians have become aware of the destructive nature of internalized homophobia and have eliminated it from their lives. They no longer believe that they are immoral and abnormal and they are not ashamed of their sexual orientation. This new attitude has helped develop a positive attitude toward homosexuality, thus improving the mental health of gays and lesbians and producing a high morale in the gay and lesbian community. Now, an increasing number of gays and lesbians love their sexual orientation and would not change it even if they could.

Examples of How Internalized Homophobia Is Harmful

- It enables the dominant group to keep gays and lesbians oppressed. *"The most potent weapon in the hands of the oppressor is the mind of the oppressed,"* according to Stephen Biko, South African revolutionary and martyr.
- It lowers self-esteem.
- It damages the spirit and prevents gays and lesbians from reaching their full potential.
- It causes gays and lesbians to hide their sexual orientation, to feel that their relationships are invalid, and to foster negative feelings toward other gays and lesbians.
- It can cause some gays and lesbians to take harmful action against other homosexuals. (It is widely believed that many

gay bashers are themselves homosexuals unable to come to terms with their sexual orientation.)

• It is a leading cause of suicide among gay teens.

• It causes self-destructive behavior, including alcoholism and substance abuse, and leads to depression and despondency.

Things to Do

• Reject society's misconceptions and stereotypes of homosexuality.

• Change your attitude from gay-negative to gay-positive.

• Begin your fight against internalized homophobia by examining and writing about how it has harmed or affected you personally. A gay friend once told me that when he was a young man he had great difficulty overcoming feelings of self-hatred. It was not until he started keeping a journal and recording and exploring his experiences that he was able to see a positive change in his self-esteem. He said that writing about his situation helped him to "clarify things," thus he was able to deal more effectively with the problem.

• Seek professional help. Counseling centers for gays and lesbians can be found in most large metropolitan areas. (Some are listed on pages 15–16.) These centers provide support and referrals to gay- and lesbian-friendly therapists. Nothing can contribute more to your struggle with internalized homophobia than a good therapist.

• Organize a discussion group with your gay and lesbian friends. Each member of the group will speak about their experience with internalized homophobia, how it has harmed them, what they are doing to eliminate it, and how their lives have improved as a result.

• List positive things about being gay or lesbian.

• You will notice that your self-esteem and mental well-being has improved since you became aware of internalized homophobia and began fighting it. List concrete examples of these improvements. For example, last night I saw two men holding hands. In the past this overt display of homosexuality would have made me uncomfortable. I would have been concerned about what heterosexuals would think about this display or how they would react. I would worry about the men's safety, and it would remind me of my own homosexuality, which was something I didn't always want to be reminded of. But now my attitude has changed and I feel happy that they have the freedom and confidence to touch in public.

• Read the literature. The Campaign to End Homophobia (see page 6) publishes a variety of pamphlets. Write and ask for a list. Titles include "Homosexuality, Heterosexism and Homophobia," "Homophobia," "I think I might be gay...now what do I do?" and "I think I might be a lesbian...now what do I do?" Also, many gays and lesbians have written books about their experience. Reading about the experiences of others will help you with yours. Suggested: *Stranger at the Gate* by Mel White (Simon & Schuster); *Same-Sex Love: and the Path to Wholeness*, edited by Robert H. Hopcke, Karin Lofthus Carrington, and Scott Wirch (Shambhala); *Being Happy Being Gay* by Bert Herrman (St. Martin's Press); and *Positively Gay: New Approaches to Gay and Lesbian Life* by Betty Berzon (Berkeley Press).

• Get involved to some degree with the gay and lesbian community in your hometown.

• Continue to reinforce your affirmative attitude toward your sexual orientation and stay optimistic about overcoming internalized homophobia.

RESOURCES

Gay and Lesbian Counseling Program
156 4th Street E

St. Paul, MN 55101
612-222-0311

Gay Men's Counseling Collective
P.O. Box 29006
Washington, DC 20017
202-265-6495

Identity House (mailing address)
P.O. Box 572 Old Chelsea Station
New York, NY 10011
212-243-8181

Iris Center
333 Valencia St., #222
San Francisco, CA 94103
415-864-2364

Montrose Counseling Center
701 Rigdeman
Houston, TX 77006
713-529-0037

Seattle Counseling Service for Sexual Minorities
200 W. Mercer St.
Seattle, WA 98119
206-282-9307

4
Learn How Personal Homophobia Is Harmful

Americans are not only less homophobic than they used to be, they are less homophobic than they think they are supposed to be.

—REP. BARNEY FRANK (D-MA)

BACKGROUND

The stigma that society places on homosexuality has negative consequences for everyone, heterosexuals included. Just as internalized homophobia is harmful to the well-being of gays and lesbians, personal homophobia is also harmful to the well-being of heterosexuals. Homophobic people develop serious character flaws that narrow their vision and place limitations on the scope of their lives. When their homophobia is put into action in the form of discrimination or violence it is destructive to society as a whole. Thus it is for your benefit and the benefit of society that you learn how it is harmful and then take action to remove it from your life.

Examples of How Personal Homophobia Is Harmful

• It inhibits intimacy between same-sex friends and family members. (This is especially true for men.) Cybill Shepherd, a supporter of gay and lesbian rights, states, "It's very important for one's mental health to get over homophobia, because at some level it's about accepting your own sex."

- It can cause you to commit crimes against gays and lesbians, and you will have to suffer the consequences of these crimes (prison or fines).
- It damages your character by making you intolerant.
- Your personal homophobia is contagious. You can infect malleable adults and children with your prejudices.
- It destroys families when a family member is ostracized for being gay or lesbian.
- It promotes a false view of reality.
- It promotes role playing, thus limiting your life and experiences.

Benefits of Ending Personal Homophobia

- It opens your mind to the variety of relations that can exist.
- It allows you to rid yourself of harmful beliefs and misinformation.
- It removes hate and the negative feelings that burden your heart and soul, and brings peace and freedom into your life.
- It makes you a nicer person.
- It has a positive impact on society as a whole.

Things to Do

- Seek out gay and lesbian friends.
- Accept sexual diversity. Remember that homosexuality is a natural and intricate part of the human condition, that it has always been and will always be as long as humanity exists.
- Get to the origin of your homophobia. Discover the immediate source. Here are some reasons why heterosexuals are homophobic:

1. Fear of being labeled gay or lesbian.
2. Belief that homosexuality is immoral and unnatural.
3. Fear of differences.
4. Belief that homosexuality is a threat to the family structure. The greatest threats to the family structure are drug and alcohol abuse, infidelity, and unemployment.

- Discuss your homophobia with a therapist.
- Participate in discussion groups on personal homophobia.
- Remember that homophobia, not homosexuality, is immoral.
- Join Parents and Friends of Lesbians and Gays (PFLAG) and develop friendships with other members of this organization. You will learn from nonhomophobic heterosexuals.
- Contribute financially to organizations that fight homophobia.
- Read gay-positive literature on homosexuality and homophobia.

RESOURCES

National Federation of Parents and Friends of Gays
8020 Eastern Ave. NW
Washington, DC 20012
202-726-3223

Parents FLAG: National Office
(Parents and Friends of Lesbians and Gays)
1101 14th Street NW, 10th Fl.
Washington, DC 20038
202-638-4200

MacLeod, Rev. Norman. "Homosexuality Is God's Gift." In *Providence Journal*, June 1, 1993.

Marcus, Eric. *Is It a Choice?* San Francisco: HarperCollins, 1993.
Mohr, Richard. *A More Perfect Union: Why Straight America Must Stand Up for Gay Rights*. Boston: Beacon Press, 1994.

5
Understand Homosexuality

Christians should affirm that homosexuality is not a curse, but a blessing to all of us, one of God's particular gifts in the created order.

REV. NORMAN MACLEOD

BACKGROUND

One significant reason for the prevalence of homophobia in American society is that a majority of Americans completely misunderstand homosexuality. For various reasons they steadfastly hold onto outmoded beliefs. Some refuse to accept facts that contradict their prejudice while others are simply unaware of the facts. The following are examples of common misconceptions about homosexuality:

• Homosexuality can be cured. The American Psychiatric Association does not include homosexuality in its list of mental disorders. If it is not an illness, how can it be cured?

• Homosexuality is contagious. Some people believe that if they or their children associate with gays or lesbians they will become homosexual. As with gays and lesbians, heterosexuals cannot change their sexual orientation or contract homosexuality from another person. However, being in the company of gays and lesbians may prompt latent homosexuals to discover and ac-knowledge their sexual orientation.

• Male homosexuality is caused by an overbearing mother and lesbianism, by an abusive father. Despite evidence to the contrary, you would be surprised how many people believe this simplistic notion. Recently researchers at the National Cancer Institute's Laboratory of Biochemistry conducted a study on gay men and reported that they had discovered a genetic component to sexual orientation. A study of DNA samples of forty pairs of gay brothers found that thirty-three of the pairs had identical pieces of a segment of chromosome. The scientists believe that a gene related to homosexuality could be located in this segment. They are currently conducting a similar study on lesbian sisters. While other studies have produced similar results, scientists and sociologists maintain that the origins and causes of sexual orien-tation are complex and subtle, involving genetic, hormonal, and environmental factors.

• Homosexuality is illegal. While it is a sorry truth that "homosexual acts" (sodomy and oral sex) are illegal in some states, homosexuality itself is not a crime.

• Homosexuality is sexual activity. Many heterosexuals and even some gays and lesbians associate homosexuality exclusively with sexual behavior. Heterosexuality, however, is never defined this way. Yet whenever I witness public displays of sexuality it is almost always between heterosexuals. Equating homosexuality with sexual activity marginalizes gays and lesbians, minimizes their relationships, and plays into the hands of the homophobes. Most gays and lesbians believe that their sexual orientation helps define who they are; it contributes to their perspective on life and shapes their attitudes. Gay and lesbian couples build a life together, give each other support, share nonsexual activities such as shopping and vacations, socialize with friends, attend cultural and sporting events, watch television, participate in political activities, and attend religious services. Some gay and lesbian couples are parents who share child-rearing responsibilities.

Things to Do

• Stay informed about what researchers are discovering about homosexuality. Subscribe to *The Journal of Homosexuality* or *The Journal of Gay and Lesbian Studies*, or visit a library and access these journals.

• If you are confused or have questions about what you read, write to the researchers for clarification.

• Assimilate this knowledge into your feelings and actions.

• Share the information with others. You can reduce or eliminate another person's homophobia just by informing them of the facts.

• Understand how homosexuality is more than sex. Challenge people who automatically equate homosexuality with sexual behavior.

• Understand that homosexuality is not a phase or an act of rebellion, and therefore it cannot be outgrown.

• Most large colleges and universities offer courses in gay and lesbian studies. Register for a course and add to your understanding of homosexuality.

• Read a book about homosexuality.

RESOURCES

Center for Lesbian and Gay Studies
c/o Duberman, CUNY Graduate Center
33 West 42nd St.
New York, NY 10036-8099
212-765-0791

Center for Research and Education in Sexuality (CERES)
San Francisco Státe University
San Francisco, CA 94132
415-338-1137

The Journal of Gay and Lesbian Studies
Gordon & Breach Publishers
International Publishers Distributor
820 Town Center Drive
Langhorne, PA 19047
800-545-8398
fax: 215-750-6343

The Journal of Homosexuality
c/o Haworth Press
10 Alice St.
Binghamton, NY 13904-1580
800-342-9678

Biery, Roger E. *Understanding Homosexuality: The Pride and the Prejudice*. Austin, TX: Edward Williams Publishing, 1990.
"Born Gay." In *Time*, July 26, 1993.
Burr, Chandler. "Homosexuality and Biology." In *The Atlantic Monthly*, March 1993.
Masters, William, and Virginia Johnson. *Homosexuality in Perspective*. Boston: Little, Brown, 1979.
McDonald, Helen B., and Audrey I. Steinhorn. *Understanding Homosexuality*. New York: Crossroad, 1993.

6
Know the History of the Gay and Lesbian Rights Movement

Gay history helps constitute the gay community by giving it a tradition, helps women and men validate and understand who they are by showing them who they have been.
                                                    — MARTIN DUBERMAN

BACKGROUND

People interested in reducing their level of homophobia will find that having some knowledge of both the history of the gay and lesbian individual in our society and the gay and lesbian rights movement provides a sense of community and belonging that contributes to unity within the group. Unity is the key ingredient for success in fighting homophobia on the political and social front. Knowledge of history gives us a sense of the past, which in turn helps us create a vision of and set a course for the future. Also, reading history is an educational tool. Educated and articulate people make effective activists, have the necessary skills for debating, advising, organizing, communicating, understanding, and dealing productively with the forces in power.

Gays and lesbians in particular will benefit from exploring the gay and lesbian experience in the past. Not only will it strengthen their understanding of their own experience, but it will give them a sense of their place in the world. In this respect, gay and lesbian history belongs to gays and lesbians.

Until the 1970s, historians and biographers were reluctant to acknowledge the sexual orientation of gays and lesbians, or study the attitudes of society, the enactment of the laws, restrictions, and all other injustices perpetrated by the dominant power against gays and lesbians. When confronted with evidence of their subject's homosexuality, some biographers simply ignored it. In *The Gay Book of Lists*, Leigh W. Rutledge reports that when Irving Stone wrote about the life of Michelangelo in *The Agony and the Ecstasy*, not once did he mention or even allude to the artist's homosexuality. Stone later denied that Michelangelo was a homosexual, claiming that the charge was "slander." Yet there is plenty of evidence pointing to the artist's sexual orientation, including love sonnets he wrote to a young nobleman. Whether or not Michelangelo's homosexuality was the driving force in his art is irrelevant. To expect the reader to understand the artist without revealing an important aspect of his being is a joke at the expense of the reader and a clear indication of active homophobia.

Fortunately, in the last twenty years, coinciding with the rise in popularity of lesbian and gay issues, historians and scholars have begun to document and analyze gays and lesbians in history. Now there is a wealth of books, journals, archives, and videos and I strongly suggest that you take advantage of this fresh and wonderful material. (The resources list I provide is only a small sample of what is available.) Both gays and nongays will enjoy reading this controversial, sometimes sad, but always colorful history.

MAJOR EVENTS IN GAY AND LESBIAN RIGHTS HISTORY

1897—Founding of Scientific Humanitarian Committee in Germany. First gay rights organization.

1950—Founding of The Mattachine Society in Los Angeles. First gay men's organization in the United States.

1955—Founding of Daughters of Bilitis in San Francisco. First lesbian organization in the United States.

1969—Stonewall Riot in Greenwich Village, turning point in the gay and lesbian rights movement.

1973—American Psychiatric Association removes homosexuality from its list of mental disorders.

1981—Center for Disease Control issues the first official warning of the forthcoming AIDS epidemic.

1993—National March on Washington for Gay, Lesbian, and Bisexual Rights.

Things to Do

• Make a commitment to learn as much as possible about gay and lesbian history.

• When reading history, use both primary sources (letters, journals of the person involved, and documents written during the era) and secondary sources (histories, biographies, and commentary written later about the era or person).

• Read literature that deals with same-gender relationships and literature written by gay and lesbian authors. The beauty of good literature is that it provides a primary source commentary on life. While the characters and plot of a great novel are fictional, the overall work provides insights into the social, political, and artistic values and practices of the era it depicts.

Suggested: *Giovanni's Room* by James Baldwin (Dell), *Nightwood* by Djuna Barnes (New Directions), *Maurice* by E. M. Forster (Vintage International), *The Well of Loneliness* by Radclyffe Hall (Bantam Doubleday), *Confessions of a Mask* by Yukio Mishima (New Directions), *Symposium* by Plato (Penguin Classics), *Poems* by Sappho (Signet Classics), *Leaves of Grass* by Walt Whitman (Penguin Classics), *Orlando* by Virginia Woolf (Harcourt Brace Jovanovich), *The City and the Pillar* by Gore Vidal (Ballantine Books).

• Keep in mind why you are reading these books and focus on the same-gender relationship or situation being depicted, the social attitudes to the situation, and the author's point of view. This will tell you something about the author.

• You can find the necessary material either in your library or a gay and lesbian bookstore.

• Visit a gay and lesbian archive.

• Rent or buy documentaries and films that deal in some way with gay and lesbian experience. If your local video store does not stock them they can be ordered through mail from Facets Video (listed in the Resources section that follows), or your local gay and lesbian bookstore will order them for you (see page 188).

RESOURCES

Blanche Baker Memorial Library and Archives (One, Inc.)
3340 Country Club Dr.
Los Angeles, CA 90019
213-735-5252

Gerber/Hart Library and Archives
3352 N. Paulina St.
Chicago, IL 60657
312-883-3003

Lesbian Herstory Archives
P.O. Box 1258
New York, NY 10116
718-768-3953

National Museum and Archive of Gay and Lesbian History
The Center
208 West 13th St.
New York, NY 10011
212-620-7310
718-726-8855 (archivist)

Quatrefoil Library
1619 Dayton Ave.
St. Paul, MN 55104
612-641-0969

Duberman, Martin, et al., eds. *Hidden from History: Reclaiming the Gay and Lesbian Past.* New York: New American Library, 1989.
———. *Stonewall.* New York: Dutton, 1993.
Faderman, Lillian. *Odd Girls and Twilight Lovers: A History of Lesbian Life in 20th Century America.* New York: Columbia University Press, 1991.
Marcus, Eric. *Making History: The Struggle for Gay and Lesbian Equal Rights: 1945–1990.* New York: HarperCollins, 1992.
Russell, Ina, ed. *Jeb and Desh: A Diary of Gay Life, 1918–1945.* New York: Faber & Faber, 1993.

Films

Before Stonewall. (1985) Directors: Greta Schiller and Robert Rosenberg

Forbidden Love. (1993) Directors: Aerlyn Weissman and Lynn Fernie

The Times of Harvey Milk. (1984) Director: Robert Epstein

Facets Video
1517 West Fullerton Ave.
Chicago, IL 60614
800-331-6197
fax: 312-929-5437
(Call for a catalog of gay and lesbian videos.)

7
Visualize a Nonhomophobic Society

Never doubt that a small group of thoughtful, committed citizens can change the world; indeed it's the only thing that ever has.

—Dr. Margaret Mead

BACKGROUND

The process of visualizing a nonhomophobic society begins with understanding the prevalence of homophobia at the present, making a commitment to change, and developing a vision for the future. Without establishing goals and a vision of the ideal future it is difficult, if not impossible, to make advances toward social reform. Having an abstract notion of what life in the future will be like for gays and lesbians is not good enough; in order to ensure that life will be better for future generations, gay and lesbian rights activists must establish a concrete view and clarify it in writing.

Some people are skeptical about the concept of visualization, calling it New Age idealism. Don't allow the negative views of others to deter you from creating your vision of a nonhomophobic society. Idealism plays a role in the work of artists; it motivates reformers to strive for the best in human nature, and even if an ideal seems impossible to achieve the process of striving for an ideal in itself brings about change.

EXAMPLE OF A VISION FOR A NONHOMOPHOBIC SOCIETY

A nonhomophobic society will benefit all people. It will be a society where freedom and justice prevails, where homosexuality will have equal status with heterosexuality, where gays and lesbians will be free to discuss their relationships and interact normally in public with their companions, as heterosexuals do now, without fearing the scorn of society, where sexual orientation is a nonissue, where, instead of putting our energies into fighting homophobia, we will focus completely on our careers, relationships, and reaching our full potential as human beings.

Things to Do

• Write a declaration of your commitment to fight homophobia.

• Put your declaration in a prominent place in your home.

• Once a month write a list of concrete things you did to fight homophobia.

• If you fail to produce a list, then you need to reaffirm your commitment.

• Write a declaration of your vision for a nonhomophobic society. This statement should reflect your values, attitudes, and beliefs for an ideal society, and include what you would eliminate from and add to the present structure. For example, "I, _____, affirm my love for humankind and respect its diversity. I recognize that gays and lesbians are valued members of society, that their sexual orientation is normal and healthy, that they should be treated with the same respect as heterosexuals, and that they should be free from fear and discrimination."

• Discuss your vision with others; perhaps they will contribute something. Encourage them to create a vision of their own.

• List the benefits of a nonhomophobic society. For example:

1. No tension between gays, lesbians, and heterosexuals.

2. No tension in families with gay and lesbian members.

3. Men would not have to continuously prove their masculinity, thus reducing levels of violence.

4. There will be no closet making it unnecessary for gays and lesbians to come out.

• Revise your vision regularly, adding or subtracting when necessary.

• Remember, creating a vision will not in itself bring change; a vision can only become reality through action.

8
Don't Live in Hiding: Come Out!

People are coming out because so much is at stake. . . . Coming out is our secret weapon.
—ROBERT BRAY, NGLTF

BACKGROUND

Because homosexuality is one of society's worst taboos, gays and lesbians were forced to conceal their sexual orientation. This hiding is called "being in the closet." Anyone who has ever concealed this basic aspect of themselves will know that being in the closet is a horrible experience. It forces gay men and lesbians to live double lives, lie to family and friends, create phony heterosexual relationships, deny their real relationships, and live with the constant fear of being found out. The closet also reinforces the homosexual taboo, contributes to the ignorance of homosexuality, and is responsible for undercounting the size of the gay and lesbian population. Coming out can be a painful process, but the benefits of living an open life cannot be denied. For example, you will eliminate subterfuge and pretense from your life, allow yourself to become a complete person, help others to understand you, and enhance your relationships with your family.

34

Disclosing your sexual orientation involves risk and is a process that you should approach thoughtfully and over a period of time. When gays and lesbians live openly they put themselves in danger of being discriminated against, of losing the love of family and friends. But they cannot allow the fear of society's disapproval and retribution to keep them imprisoned in the closet. They must acknowledge and accept the risks involved and come out cautiously, using good judgment and the support systems available in the gay and lesbian community.

Today more and more gay and lesbian people, including celebrities, are taking a brave step and coming out. An old friend from my high school days, whom I hadn't seen since graduation and who ended our friendship when I told her I was a lesbian, recently called me up and said she wanted to talk. We met and she came out to me. It was a healing experience. The irony of the situation was not lost on us and we had a good laugh. She was living in the closet for years, decided that she couldn't stand it anymore, and began the coming-out process. The single most important thing you can do to fight homophobia is to come out to your family, friends, and perhaps your coworkers, and live as a proud, openly gay or lesbian person.

You Should Know

• Forty-six percent of Americans say they do not know a gay or lesbian person. The same survey shows that the 54 percent who know someone who is gay or lesbian are less homophobic and tend to support gay and lesbian rights legislation.

• Recently, some famous people to come out of the closet include singers k.d. lang, Elton John, Melissa Etheridge, Janis Ian, and Boy George, TV journalist Steve Gendel, tennis star Martina Navratilova, architect Philip Johnson, TV actress (*Married With Children*) Amanda Bearse, entertainer Sandra Bernhard, and producer David Geffen.

Things to Do

• Come out at your own pace. Don't allow others to pressure you into coming out too quickly.

• Before coming out to your family, establish a support system by discussing it with a trusted friend or, even better, a gay- and lesbian-positive counselor.

• Participate in a coming-out discussion group at your local gay and lesbian center.

• Read pamphlets dealing with coming out. You will find them at gay and lesbian bookstores or community centers, or write or call PFLAG (page 19).

• Read gay- and lesbian-positive literature dealing with the coming-out experience, including coming-out stories by other gays and lesbians.

• Choose a safe and comfortable setting to come out to your family.

• Choose a time when you and your family are free from tension or anger.

• Approach the discussion with a positive attitude about your sexuality.

• It is a good idea to rehearse what you are going to say and how you are going to say it. Write it down and read it aloud to yourself beforehand.

• Prepare your family by letting them know that you have something important to tell them.

• Be patient. Give your family members time to adjust to this news. They may have to go through a process that will include shock, denial, guilt, and acceptance.

• Inform your family about PFLAG and suggest that they contact this organization.

• Use your judgment. If you are a young person living at home and dependent on your parents and they are homophobic and prejudiced people who will probably react to you in a hurtful way, then it is better not to come out to them at this time. Wait until you have finished school and are self-sufficient.

• Come out to *all* your friends. A true friend will accept you for who you are; the others you can do without.

• Should you lose a friend when you come out, replace him or her with an accepting and understanding person.

• Join National Coming Out Day (October 11) and request educational information. National Coming Out Day serves as a reminder that you need to begin or continue the process of coming out.

Coming Out in the Workplace

• Some gay men and lesbians feel it is unnecessary to come out to everyone at work and disclose their sexual orientation only to coworker friends or people who ask, or to gay or lesbian coworkers. Coming out in the workplace could cost you your job; therefore, if your company has a homophobic or reactionary atmosphere, be extremely cautious and make realistic judgments about who, if anyone, you can tell.

• Many large corporations have gay and lesbian employee support groups. If one exists in your company, make contact and participate.

• Find out your employer's attitude toward gays and lesbians before you decide to come out. Does your company include sexual orientation in its nondiscrimination policy?

• Before coming out in the workplace, contact NGLTF Workplace Project for a consultation.

RESOURCES

National Coming Out Day
P.O. Box 34640
Washington, DC 20043-4640
800-866-NCOD

National Gay and Lesbian Task Force
Workplace Project
2320 17th St.
Washington, DC 20009
202-332-6483
fax: 202-332-0207

Barber, Karen, and Sarah Holmes, eds. *Testimonies: Lesbian Coming-Out Stories*. Boston: Alyson, 1994.

Eichberg, Rob. *Coming Out: An Act of Love*. New York: Plume, 1991.

"Coming Out to Your Parents" by T. H. Sauerman (pamphlet). Contact PFLAG (page 19) for copies.

McNaught, Brian. *Gay Issues in the Workplace*. New York: St. Martin's Press, 1993.

Monette, Paul. *Becoming a Man*. San Francisco: Harper/SF, 1992.

Muchmore, Wes, and William Hanson. *Coming Out Right: A Handbook for the Gay Male*. Boston: Alyson, 1993.

Saks, Adrien, and Wayne Curtis, eds. *Revelations: Gay Men's Coming-Out Stories*. Boston: Alyson, 1994.

Signorile, Michelangelo. *Queer in America*. New York: Random House, 1993.

9
Support Family and Friends Coming Out

BACKGROUND

Many parents are devastated when they discover that their child is gay or lesbian. Some reject their children outright, disown and disinherit them. Others experience a process that begins with rejection, evolves through feelings of anger, remorse, hostility, and guilt, and arrives at understanding and open acceptance. The process of coming to terms with a child's homosexuality is difficult for everyone involved, and it's important for parents to find information and support that does not add to their fears and concerns. Fortunately there is a wealth of information available, including books, pamphlets, and support groups, such as Parents and Friends of Lesbians and Gays (PFLAG). It is important to realize that you do not have to go through this process alone, that thousands of parents before you have had a similar experience, and some are available to give you the support and information necessary for you and your son or daughter to survive with your relationship intact.

Friends of gays and lesbians also have to undergo a process when a friend comes out to them. Many people will suspect that their friend is gay or lesbian and are relieved when it is finally out and discussed. Then the friendship will begin to develop and grow in a new level. When people are shocked at discovering that their friend is gay or lesbian they may justifiably question the quality of the friendship. How could it have been a true friendship when such a fundamental aspect of the friend's persona remained hidden? It is important not to dwell too much on this issue because it could prevent the friendship from moving forward. Accept the person's disclosure of sexual orientation as a positive development for your friendship.

Things to Do

PARENTS AND FAMILIES

• Reaffirm your love for your son or daughter. Unconditional love is the most important thing your child needs after coming out.

• Be supportive. It is your responsibility as a parent to be there for your child. Let him or her know that coming out was the right thing to do.

• Remember that your gay son or lesbian daughter is the same person he or she was before coming out.

• Give yourself time to adjust to the news.

• Keep the lines of communication open. Ask as many questions as you want and listen to what your son or daughter says, encouraging them to discuss their feelings with you.

• Teenagers have special needs that should be addressed. Contact a gay or lesbian youth services organization, PFLAG, or a gay- and lesbian-positive therapist to get the necessary information on how to help him or her cope.

• Develop a positive atmosphere around this issue and celebrate your child's sexual orientation by understanding the difficulties he or she faces, speaking out against homophobia, and helping other family members to be accepting.

- Avoid turning the disclosure into a family crisis.
- Be as proud of your gay son or daughter's relationship as you are of the relationships with your heterosexual children.
- Teach heterosexual children to respect their gay and lesbian siblings and schoolmates.
- Become a role model for other parents coming to terms with having gay or lesbian children.

FRIENDS

- Don't assume that your gay or lesbian friend knows that you are supportive. Tell them and encourage them in their coming-out process.
- Discuss your reservations and concerns with your gay or lesbian friend. As in all relationships, a good level of communication solves problems and resolves misunderstandings.
- Some heterosexuals believe that gays and lesbians are attracted to everyone of the same gender. Don't make this mistake and don't think that when a gay or lesbian friend of the same gender comes out to you they are making a pass. This type of reaction can destroy friendships.
- Celebrate diversity and rejoice in having a gay or lesbian friend.

RESOURCES

Lambda Youth and Family Empowerment (LYFE)
Call Laura or Howard at 415-359-0207 for more information on this group.

PFLAG
1012 14th St. NW #700
Washington, DC 20005
202-638-4200

Cohen, Susan and Daniel. *When Someone You Know Is Gay.*
New York: Dell, 1988.

Fairchild, Betty, and Nancy Hayward. *Now That You Know:
What Every Parent Should Know About Homosexuality.* New
York: Harvest, 1993.

Griffin, Carolyn and Marian, and Arthur G. Wirth. *Beyond Acceptance: Parents of Lesbians and Gays Talk About Their Experiences.* New Jersey: Prentice-Hall, 1986.

10
Find Positive Gay and Lesbian Role Models

I want the kids to know that there are plenty of people who are
successful, happy, and gay.
— DOYLE FORISTER, GAY TEACHER

BACKGROUND

It is natural for young people to seek out individuals with whom they can identify, whose lives and achievements they recognize and admire. Usually they find role models within their own family, but many situations exist where the family cannot provide adequate role models and young people must search outside for guidance. This is often the case for gay and lesbian youth. Therefore it is vital that positive gay and lesbian role models be available to help young people overcome internalized homophobia and isolation, build self-esteem, and be proud of their sexual orientation.

The most important criterion for someone to be a positive role model is that they live positive, healthy lives, have a good set of values, contribute something to the community, completely accept their sexual orientation and, most important, are out of the closet. In the past, gay and lesbian youth had a difficult time finding positive gay and lesbian role models. The stigma was so powerful that almost everyone was closeted, and when homosexual characters were depicted in movies or literature they represented negative stereotypes, usually coming to a bad end.

Fortunately today there is an abundance of people who are out, visible, and dedicated to establishing a strong, viable gay and lesbian community. There are gay and lesbian role models to be found in all walks of life, allowing gay and lesbian youth to explore all aspects of what society has to offer, to free themselves from stereotypes, and to expand their horizons. Some role models are regular, unsung individuals who represent the core of the community and others are famous and openly gay or lesbian, like Larry Kramer and Martina Navratilova, whose talent and accomplishments have put them in the national spotlight.

SOME FAMOUS ROLE MODELS

Politics: Barney Frank (D-MA), Tom Duane (City Council, NYC), Deborah Glick (NYS Assembly), Harvey Milk , Roberta Achtenberg (HUD appointee), Richard Taffel (Executive director of Log Cabin Federation).

Arts and Entertainment: Jerry Herman (composer), Kate Clinton (comedian), Ian McKellen (actor), Melissa Etheridge (musician), k. d. lang (musician), Janis Ian (musician), Audre Lorde (poet), Tony Kushner (playwright), Vito Russo (film historian), Randy Shilts (writer), David Leavitt (writer), Amanda Bearse (actress), Jewelle Gomez (writer), Philip Johnson (architect), Steve Gendel (journalist).

Activists: Larry Kramer, Michelangelo Signorile, Joyce Hunter, Frank Kameny, Ann Northrop, Suzanne Pharr, Marjorie Hill, and David Mixner.

Business: Judy Dlugacz (president of Olivia Records and Cruises), and David Geffen.

HETEROSEXUALS TO ADMIRE

Governor William Weld (R-MA) is a supporter of gay and lesbian rights. Barry Goldwater spoke out publicly against homophobia and criticized his own party (Republican) for embracing organizations such as the Christian Coalition. Cybill Shepherd fights homophobia and attended the 1993 gay and lesbian march on Washington. Elizabeth Taylor is a dedicated AIDS activist. Tom Hanks was the first major Hollywood star to risk his career and give an honest and nonstereotypical portrait of a gay man in the movie *Philadelphia*. Hanks won an Academy Award for this role.

Things to Do

• Gay and lesbian youth should seek out a gay or lesbian role model whose work and life they relate to and admire.

• Discuss your role models with friends and why they impact your life. This will help clarify your values and goals to yourself and your friends.

• Educate others about setting a good example and becoming a role model.

• Be your own role model. Be true to yourself and live in a way that makes you proud of your accomplishments and values.

• Reach out to young people, become a role model, and offer them your support and guidance. The availability of gay and lesbian role models helps prevent homosexual youth from becoming homophobic and feeling isolated. It also reveals the positive aspects of being part of the gay and lesbian community. Remember, some young people can easily be influenced by adults and as open-minded, mature adults it is our responsibility not to take advantage of this vulnerability by setting a good example.

• Volunteer at a gay and lesbian youth organization. Organize and lead a discussion group for young gays and lesbians, focusing on topics like safe sex, social intercourse, coping with homophobia, coming out, and antigay and lesbian violence.

RESOURCES

Boston Alliance of Gay and Lesbian Youth (BAGLY)
P.O. Box 814
Boston, MA 02103
800-422-2459

Center Youth Enrichment Services (YES)
c/o Lesbian and Gay Community Services Center
208 West 13th St.
New York, NY 10011
212-620-7310

Hetrick-Martin Institute
2 Astor Pl.
New York, NY 10003
212-674-2400
fax: 212-674-8650

National Youth Network
P.O. Box 846
San Francisco, CA 94101

Sexual Minority Youth Assistance League (SMYAL)
333 1/2 Pennsylvania Ave. SE
Washington, DC 20003-1148
202-546-5911
Bulletin and helpline

11
Use Nonhomophobic Language

Speech is a mirror of the soul: as a man speaks, so is he.
—SYRUS

BACKGROUND

Language is the verbal expression of ideas and a tool for people to understand and portray the universe. From the distinct and intertwined relationship between language and ideas emerges the power of words. Words have meaning and therefore are a powerful weapon that members of society use for both positive and negative reasons. In recent centuries, the dominant group, heterosexuals, has taken advantage of this weapon to stigmatize and ostracize gays and lesbians. Homosexuality and lesbianism were defined by terms like *perversion*, *abnormal*, and *deviance*, and since gays and lesbians engaged in relationships that others deemed unacceptable they were ridiculed with words like *faggot*, *dyke*, and *queer* and were expected to feel shame and hide their sexual orientation.

Although reactionaries still describe homosexuality in negative terms, they seem to be in the minority and many people, gay and straight, accept it as a normal, important, and intricate part of the human experience. This new attitude emerges from the success of the gay and lesbian rights movement and language reform has played an important role. By rejecting words like *pervert* and reclaiming others like *queer* and giving them new and positive meanings, reformers have helped create change and improved the quality of life for gays and lesbians. Reclaiming words that are considered derogatory is called *stigma conversion*. It is a controversial issue within the gay and lesbian rights movement. The more conservative or mainstream gays and lesbians have expressed their discomfort over being defined as *queer*, *fag*, or *dyke*, especially in a mainstream setting. Others feel that these words belong to them, that a homophobic society attached the stigma and the process of reclaiming and controlling language is empowering and turns the tables on the homophobes. In the long run, it is up to you as an individual to define who you are.

As with all change, language reform is an ongoing, refining process that requires understanding and perseverance. New words and definitions may seem appropriate initially, but time and continuous change determines whether the word is useful. For example, in the early 1970s *gay* became a blanket term for both men and women. Lesbians working quickly to change this insisted on using *lesbian*. They felt that as women if they were defined by a term that also defines a man they would become even less visible than they already are. Anyway, they felt *lesbian* is a powerful word with a sense of history that invokes the great poet Sappho, the mother of all lesbians. What could be more perfect? Yet this word was underused as a result of the-love-that-dare-not-speak-its-name mentality and it needed to be dusted off and given its proper place.

You Should Know

• The expression *gay lifestyle* is homophobic. There is no gay lifestyle just as there is no heterosexual lifestyle. Lifestyle is determined by class and economic differences, not sexual orientation.

• While gays and lesbians often call each other *queers*, *fags*, or *dykes*, they consider it homophobic and offensive when heterosexuals use these words.

Things to Do

• Understand and accept that gays and lesbians are a diverse group and thus will define themselves differently. You can avoid embarrassing or hurtful situations by asking your gay and lesbian friends what words they prefer you to use if you are unsure.

• You can weaken the connection between oppression and language when you avoid using words that describe homosexuality in negative terms.

• If you are struggling with personal or internalized homophobia, focus your energy on controlling the language of your thoughts. If you don't think it, then you won't feel it. You will find that this mental exercise will reinforce your use of nonhomophobic language and therefore help to reduce your homophobia.

• Use *sexual orientation* instead of *sexual preference*. *Preference* implies that gays and lesbians made a conscious decision to be homosexual.

• *Companion* is the acceptable term for heterosexuals to use when describing the partner of a gay or lesbian. While some gays and lesbians still like to use *lover*, it's inappropriate in political or mainstream situations because it only defines the sexual aspect of the relationship.

• Most gay men prefer *gay* to *homosexual*, feeling that homosexual is a cold, clinical word.

• Inform heterosexuals when they use homophobic language, but be careful not to alienate by using a hostile tone.

They may be unaware that their words are offensive and just need to be told.

• Don't dismiss nonhomophobic language as a politically correct euphemism. Gays and lesbians are changing the negative language that society uses to define them and are defining themselves in a way they feel is correct.

• Remember that positive language elevates.

RESOURCES

Dynes, Wayne. *Homolexis: A Historical and Cultural Lexicon of Homosexuality.* New York: Gai Saber, 1985.
Marcus, Eric. "What's in a Name?" In *10 Percent*, Winter 1993.

12
Participate in Gay Pride Week Events

There's a certain comfort in being among so many people who have all experienced self-discoveries similar to one's own, and who have all had to deal with the same slights and cruelties. . . .

—BRUCE BAWER

BACKGROUND

Gay Pride Week commemorates the June 28, 1969, Stonewall Riot in New York City. On that day, patrons in Stonewall, a gay and lesbian bar, rioted when the police raided the bar and tried to arrest them. The riot lasted for three days and marked a turning point in the struggle for gay and lesbian rights. Until this time rights activists protested quietly and received little attention from the media and other gays and lesbians. The Stonewall uprising, with its forcefulness, spontaneity, and success as an act of defiance, demonstrated to police and politicians that gays and lesbians had reached the saturation point and no longer intended to peacefully endure the harassment and injustices they had endured for centuries. The media now began to take notice, and gays and lesbians around the country took the call to action and began coming out, organizing, and marching for justice on a scale much greater than before. The modern gay and lesbian civil rights struggle was born that week in June 1969 in New York City.

Each year gays and lesbians commemorate Stonewall with weeklong events of celebration that culminate on the last Sunday of June with the Gay Pride March. Stonewall commemorations reinforce bonds between gays and lesbians, remind them and their supporters that their struggle for civil rights continues, that they should stay united, and honor heros, past and present. For most gays and lesbians it is an exhilarating experience that augments their sense of pride and struggle. It provides the visibility that the heterosexual world needs to witness, and informs heterosexuals that gays and lesbians are proud of who they are and don't intend to regress to the closet. Yes, there is controversy around the issues of how gays and lesbians should present themselves to the world on Gay Pride Day. Whatever side of the issue you take it should not prevent you from participating in the march and showing up for Gay and Lesbian Pride Week. If you have strong opinions about how the march should be organized, then become involved with the march's planning committee and do your best to advance your ideas, but boycotting the march is counterproductive for the common and ultimate cause that depends not only on unity but the strength, visibility, power, and security that arises from a mass assembly.

While Gay Pride Week appeals mainly to gays, lesbians, and bisexuals, heterosexuals should and are welcome to participate. A civil rights struggle must receive the support of all people concerned with civil rights. Some heterosexuals have, for one reason or another, been denied their civil rights and know the consequences; they can strengthen their own position by helping to secure the rights of others. In addition, special groups like PFLAG provide a place for heterosexuals who have close relationships, family, and friendships with gays and lesbians to demonstrate their support.

Did You Know

• Almost 2 million people participated in gay and lesbian pride marches in cities and towns throughout the United States in 1993.

• Marches and other events are held not only in the United States, but also in some major European cities.

Things to Do

• Make a commitment to either march in the parade or view it from the sidelines.

• Volunteer to be a marshal for the march.

• If you have a companion, the Gay and Lesbian Pride March is a good opportunity to publicly demonstrate affection and not be concerned about harassment.

• Show your pride and identification with the movement by displaying the symbols of the movement. Wear something lavender and carry the rainbow flag.

• If you haven't yet chosen a gay or lesbian organization to join, find a group with which you identify, march with them, and contribute to their celebration.

• Unaffiliated individuals can also participate in Gay Pride Week events.

• Don't limit your participation to just the march. Especially if you live in a large city you will find a variety of events taking place during Gay and Lesbian Pride Week that you should attend and support. For example, annual events in New York's celebration include The Garden Party, the Lesbian Pride Dance, the rally on the evening before the march, the Gay and Lesbian Heritage Walking Tour, Lesbian and Gay Pride Run, Pride Festival, Fireworks, and Gay Pride Worship Services.

• Inform family and friends (gay and straight) about the events and march, and encourage them to participate.

• Design and construct a placard to display the slogans of the movement.

• Watch mainstream media coverage of Gay and Lesbian Pride Month, and also encourage your family and friends to watch.

• Gay and lesbian organizations in large cities publish pride guides and other publications relating to pride week. Volunteer and help them produce these publications.

• If you own a business, support the pride publications with advertising.

• Gays and lesbians living in rural areas may not have a pride celebration in their area. Many travel to the nearest city to participate. Those who don't want to make a trip and want a local celebration of pride week should organize their own event in their home and start a grassroots organization devoted to pride week.

• Be proud all year, not just during Gay Pride Week.

RESOURCES

Heritage of Pride, Inc.
208 West 13th St.
New York, NY 10011
212-80-PRIDE

Houston Lesbian and Gay Pride Week
P.O. Box 66701
Houston, TX 77266
713-529-6979

Lesbian and Gay Pride Week Planning Committee
P.O. Box 14131
Chicago, IL 60614
312-348-8243

Arizona Lesbian and Gay Pride Committee
P.O. Box 26139
Tempe, AZ 85285
602-352-7165

The Pride Guide
Pride Publishing, Inc.
80 Eighth Avenue, Suite 902
New York, NY 10011
212-807-9839
fax: 212-807-9843

13
Emphasize the Positive

BACKGROUND

There are many consequences of forcing gays and lesbians to hide their sexual orientation. Society becomes ignorant of homosexuality and the lives of gays and lesbians, allowing homophobic people to infect society with their negative views. The majority embraced this perspective for centuries and was willing to accept homosexuality as a dark and shady aspect of humanity that they had to suppress, resulting in the dehumanization of gays and lesbians. To protect themselves from oppression most gays and lesbians lived a closeted life in which no one but their dearest friends and lovers knew their true nature. This invisibility made it easy for homophobic people to perpetuate the myth that gays and lesbians had nothing positive to contribute to society. Little did they know that some of the people they respected as individuals or whose accomplishments society recognized were gay and lesbian.

People working to make life better for gays and lesbians

have confronted the negativity that surrounds homosexuality. Attitudes began to change when gays and lesbians came out of the closet and demonstrated to open-minded heterosexuals that there was nothing to fear. Counteracting the negative can be accomplished by emphasizing the positive. By not accepting the distorted impressions that the dominant group puts forth and illustrating through personal example the positive aspects of being gay or lesbian, eventually the negativity that homophobic people promote will fade. This is accomplished by first reevaluating the prevailing beliefs about homosexuality, understanding the bigotry and cynicism behind them, and then emphasizing to yourself, friends, family, and coworkers the positive contributions and aspects of being gay or lesbians.

Examples

• Being gay, lesbian, or bisexual is natural, normal, and healthy.

• Homosexuality exists in every race, religion, and class. Scientists have even observed homosexual behavior in some animal species.

• Gays and lesbians participate in all professions. There are gay and lesbian bankers, lawyers, doctors, artists, writers, scientists, soldiers, police officers, politicians, actors, chefs, managers, waiters, preachers, and teachers.

• Many gay and lesbian couples develop nurturing, loving, and monogamous relationships. Although no studies have been done on the average length of gay and lesbian relationships, I personally know male and female couples who have been together for many years.

• Despite the prejudice directed against them, most gays and lesbians are strong and determined enough to rise above the destruction of homophobia and live as normal, well-adjusted, law-abiding citizens.

• Openly gay and lesbian people are courageous and should be commended for their honesty and bravery.

• Looking at history, you will find gays and lesbians among the world's most accomplished and prominent citizens. Renowned historical figures who were gay, lesbian, or bisexual include:

Sappho (c.600 B.C.) Greek poet

Socrates (c.470 B.C.) Greek philosopher

Alexander the Great (356–323 B.C.) Greek military leader

Leonardo da Vinci (1452–1519) Italian painter and inventor

Queen Christina (1626–1689) Swedish monarch

Walt Whitman (1819–1892) American poet

Oscar Wilde (1854–1900) Irish writer

Marcel Proust (1871–1922) French writer

Willa Cather (1873–1947) American writer

Gertrude Stein (1874–1946) American writer and poet

E. M. Forster (1879–1970) English writer

Bessie Smith (1894–1937) American singer

Greta Garbo (1905–1990) American actress, born in Sweden

Tennessee Williams (1911–1983) American playwright

James Baldwin (1924–1987) American writer

Yukio Mishima (1925–1970) Japanese writer

Things to Do

• Make your own list of positive aspects of being gay or lesbian.

• Focus on the positive features within yourself or your gay and lesbian friends.

• Compare your life and experiences with the negative representations of gays and lesbians you encounter. By comparing your life or the lives of your gay or lesbian friends to these representations, you can demonstrate to yourself and others that the negativity is grounded in homophobia.

- Avoid reinforcing negative stereotypes.
- Challenge homophobic people to say something positive about gays and lesbians.
- Know about the contributions of gays and lesbians to society. Should you have difficulty finding information on this subject, go to a gay and lesbian bookstore.
- Remain vigilant. Homophobia is widespread and can be contagious; you will constantly encounter negative feelings toward gays and lesbians. You can prevent homophobia from infiltrating your thoughts by reinforcing and emphasizing your positive attitude.

RESOURCES

Russell, Paul. *The Gay 100: A Ranking of the Most Influential Gay Men and Lesbians, Past and Present.* New York: Citadel Press, 1995.

14
Learn How Interpersonal Homophobia Is Harmful

BACKGROUND

Interpersonal homophobia occurs when personal and internalized homophobia materializes in the behavior of individuals who act out their prejudice by means of negative or criminal conduct directed against gays and lesbians or the community. The degree to which someone engages in antigay and lesbian behavior depends on how damaged they are by homophobia. The active component can manifest in forms ranging from verbal abuse, demeaning jokes, name-calling, distributing propaganda, and discrimination to acts of violence. One likes to believe that people who engage in homophobic behavior are the most ignorant and unenlightened people, and many are, yet how does one explain the likes of Ernest Hemingway—educated, creative, and a notorious homophobe. In *Hemingway: A Life Without Consequences*, the biographer, James Mellow, discusses Hemingway's homophobia. He states: "Hemingway despised male homosexuals throughout his life." Mellow reports incidents when Hemingway used name-calling to ridicule gay men. After Hemingway had a falling out with his friend Gertrude Stein he attacked her sexuality in *A Moveable Feast*. One could theorize that Hemingway experienced homosexual desires that repulsed him and that he acted out this internalized homophobia by disparaging homosexuals. Whatever the reason, everyone, whether straight or gay, has at some point done or said something that was motivated by their homophobia.

One success in the struggle for the dignity of gays and lesbians is that obvious homophobic behavior is considered unacceptable in mainstream, polite company; therefore some homophobes find it necessary to hide their true feelings and express them only in the presence of heterosexuals from whom they expect support. A friend of mine who works for a progressive corporation in New York City has heard professionals make nasty, homophobic comments when they thought gay and lesbian coworkers were not present. Even if homophobes are careful to conceal their homophobia around gays and lesbians, expressing it in any setting keeps it alive and instills it into the thoughts of others, causing harm to everyone.

An important step to take in eliminating interpersonal homophobia is to know how it is harmful to gays, lesbians, heterosexuals, and society in general:

• It can and often does result in physical assaults on gays and lesbians, damaging their physical, psychological, and emotional well-being.

• The threat of violence, verbal abuse, or discrimination causes some gays and lesbians to live in fear and paranoia, to curb their normal activities, and to hide a vital part of who they are as people.

• Interpersonal homophobia can prevent gays and lesbians accused of crimes from receiving a fair trial.

• Gay and lesbian bashing compromises the fundamental

decency of the basher and can result in a prison term that is harmful to the basher and burdensome to society.

• Homophobic expression reveals to gays and lesbians that some people consider them to be second-class citizens. Many unenlightened gays and lesbians are vulnerable to this message and start to believe it, thus damaging their self-esteem.

• Interpersonal homophobia can divide families if a homophobic parent discovers that their child is gay or lesbian.

• It forces men and women into rigid and stifling role playing.

• The threat of being called a "dyke" is used against heterosexual women to keep them in their place. I have heard men dismiss Hillary Clinton and Janet Reno as "dykes." The National Organization for Women has acknowledged that in the past feminists who feared the label "lesbian" curtailed their involvement in the feminist movement.

• The threat of being called a "fag" prevents heterosexual men from sharing intimate feelings or sensual interaction and causes the obnoxious behavior that results from hypermasculinity.

Things to Do

• Acknowledge and list instances when you have engaged in homophobic behavior. Remember, examples include name-calling and offensive jokes directed toward gays and lesbians.

• Gays and lesbians must also acknowledge and list their homophobic behavior.

• For each item on your list understand how it harmed you and others.

• List incidents when you have been victimized by homophobia. This list can be compiled by gays, lesbians, and heterosexuals. Recently, a heterosexual friend of mine was called a "dyke" because she rejected a man's sexual advances.

• Include in your list where and when the incident took place, your age at that time, any events that led up to the incident, and how you responded.

• Explore your feelings around each incident, how it affected your self-esteem, emotional and physical well-being, how it has affected your life, and how you coped.

• Encourage a friend to make a similar list and then compare items and responses.

RESOURCES

"Homophobia: Discrimination Based on Sexual Orientation." Booklet produced by GLAAD/LA, 1991.

Israel, Constance Denny. *Hate Crimes Against Gays/Lesbians*. Las Colinas, TX: Monument Press, 1992.

Pharr, Suzanne. *Homophobia: A Weapon of Sexism*. Little Rock, AR: Chardon Press, 1988.

Signorile, Michelangelo. *Queer in America*. New York: Random House, 1993.

15
Report All Gay and Lesbian Bashing Incidents

BACKGROUND

The number of reported incidents of antigay and lesbian violence and harassment has increased in recent years. In order to deal effectively with this rise in violence and prevent it from occurring, gays and lesbians must take action. Without a response, gay and lesbian bashers will get the message that they can commit bias crimes with impunity. The first step is to report *all* incidents to local police, the National Gay and Lesbian Task Force Anti-Violence Project, the Hate Crimes Hotline, and the antiviolence project in your community. Official records and statistics demonstrate to law enforcement agencies, including police and judiciary, and to politicians that hate crimes committed against gays and lesbians are a major problem that they need to address. Through your activism, letter writing, demonstrating, and political action, you will influence the way law enforcement officials and politicians deal with bias crimes.

Not only gays and lesbians, but heterosexuals also should

express outrage at and become involved in the fight against anti-gay or lesbian violence. Heterosexuals too are victimized by hate crimes and there are cases where heterosexuals mistaken for gay have been physically assaulted. Of course, a sense of human decency and fairness should be the prime motivation for combating hate crime, but self-interest will do when these feelings are absent. In addition, it is important to realize that, while the perpetrators should and must be punished and rehabilitated, they too are victims of this society's intrinsic homophobia and of their own ignorance, which has been exploited by powerful and unscrupulous homophobic forces such as the Christian Coalition, the Catholic Church, and other such organizations.

You Should Know

The senate in a 95-4 vote approved the Federal Hate Crimes Enhancement Act of 1993. The hate crimes bill lengthens sentences for federal crimes if they are proven to be motivated by hatred of a victim's race, religion, color, national origin, gender, disability, or sexual orientation. The four senators who voted against the act were Launch Faircloth (R-NC), Russell Feingold (D-WI), Jesse Helms (R-NC), and Malcolm Wallop (R-WY).

Things to Do

• Stay alert and use prevention as a defense. Some incidents can be avoided with quick thinking and by trusting your instincts.

• Learn basic self-defense skills, stay physically fit, and fight back. Self-defense is a basic right so don't be afraid to defend yourself by whatever means necessary.

• If you live in a rural or gay- and lesbian-unfriendly area, you should form phone trees with other gays and lesbians and develop a plan of action when or if someone is bashed. Also organize support groups that distribute important information about local homophobes, antigay attitudes, and incidents of harassment and violence.

• Volunteer at anti-violence projects.

• Write to your local police force encouraging sensitivity training for all officers.

• Lobby lawmakers to enact laws that protect gays and lesbians from hate crimes, both on the state and local level.

• Be a good citizen. If you witness a bias attack, come forward and testify.

• If you know someone who has victimized gays or lesbians, talk to them about their problem and encourage them to seek counseling.

IF YOU ARE ATTACKED

• Report it.

• There is a course of action that you should take if you have been victimized. The NGLTF Anti-Violence Project has a guide that discusses self-defense, getting help, dealing with law enforcement agencies, and community organizing. This pamphlet costs $4.

• Immediately following the incident write a detailed account of what happened: facts, dates, witnesses, what was said, details of injuries, and law enforcement response.

• In order to overcome emotional or psychological injury incurred as the result of an attack, seek professional counseling.

• Sue the bashers. In addition to the criminal case, pursue a civil case if you have the resources.

• Participate in demonstrations against bias crime.

• Your best revenge is to turn this negative experience into a positive one. Use it as motivation to become involved in educating yourself and others about hate crimes and how to fight against violence. You can receive all the necessary information from the NGLTF Anti-Violence Project.

• Use this information to organize on a grassroots level. Plan a meeting in your home with other victims of antigay and lesbian violence and discuss constructive activism.

• Get involved in community education programs and give a face to antigay and lesbian violence by speaking at schools and churches about your experience.

• Write a letter to your political representatives informing them about your experience, how it has affected your life, and what you want them to do.

RESOURCES

Hate Crimes National Hotline
U.S. Department of Justice
Constitution Ave. & 10th St. NW
Washington, DC 20530
800-347-HATE
202-514-2000

New York City Gay and Lesbian Anti-Violence Project
647 Hudson St.
New York, NY 10014
212-807-6761
24-hour hotline: 212-807-0197

The Center for Anti-Violence Education
421 5th Ave.
Brooklyn, NY 11215
718-788-1775

National Gay and Lesbian Task Force Anti-Violence Project
1734 14th St. NW
Washington, DC 20009
202-332-6483
fax: 202-332-0207

National Victims Center
309 W. 7th St. #705
Ft. Worth, TX 76102
817-877-3355

Comstock, G. *Violence Against Lesbians and Gay Men.* New York: Columbia University Press, 1991.
Herek, Gregory. *Bashers, Baiters, and Bigots: Homophobia in American Society.* New York: Harrington Park Press, 1985.

16
When Challenged, Defend Your Sexual Orientation

BACKGROUND

Gays and lesbians are often put on the defensive by people who make casual homophobic remarks, hurl blatant insults, or challenge them with misinformation and distorted facts. While gays and lesbians prefer not to have to defend their sexual orientation, they must respond when confronted, if the situation allows. The main reason for responding to verbal attacks and homophobic assumptions is to turn it around, to transform a negative into a positive experience. An effective response to these remarks can prompt the homophobes to reeducate themselves, question their beliefs, and explore the facts, and it protects the pride and self-esteem of gays and lesbians who refuse to remain passive while their feelings are getting hurt and their sense of well-being violated. Also, responding cautiously to verbal attacks reduces the level of anger such incidents can provoke in gays and lesbians.

Responding to verbal attacks is tricky and should be done

using caution and instincts. Each situation is unique and requires an appropriate response that only good judgment and quick thinking can provide. Since verbal attacks are often the prelude to physical assaults, it is important to determine before you respond whether or not the possibility of violence exists. Some activists feel that gays and lesbians should join the fray and always respond regardless of the possibility of violence. I, however, encourage you to remove yourself quickly from the scene if you sense violence, if the homophobe is intoxicated, or if you are outnumbered. The following are possible settings in which verbal attacks can take place:

• An acquaintance or friend makes a casual homophobic comment or reinforces a stereotype. In this situation, it is unlikely that the offender intends to follow through with a physical attack and you should make an assertive response and reprimand.

• An acquaintance or stranger deliberately insults you with a blatant homophobic remark. While there is always the possibility of violence when dealing with strangers in these instances, a calm and logical response could be effective.

• A stranger hurls a homophobic insult and threatens you with violence. If you cannot resist a response, then be prepared to run or fight. Fight only if you are physically fit, feeling brave, have self-defense training, and are not outnumbered. Your self-confidence and unwillingness to back down will probably prompt the homophobe to retreat.

• Keeping in mind that the reason for responding is to turn a negative into a positive, ask yourself if anything positive can be accomplished. If the answer is no, then walk away and deal with the injury to your pride by discussing it with friends or a therapist.

• Heterosexuals who witness a verbal attack on a gay or lesbian should speak up. Their assistance could help to defuse the situation. The taunter may retreat when bystanders intervene and the victim is encouraged to know that he or she does not have to stand alone. I remember an incident that occurred a few years ago. While waiting for a bus, I became the victim of a homophobic verbal attack by two teenage boys. Before I had a chance to respond a straight couple standing near me came to my defense. Using a loud, aggressive tone of voice, the man told the teens to "get lost"; the woman also spoke up, telling them that they should be ashamed. The teens quietly walked away. Although I still felt humiliated and angry, I was grateful to the couple for their support. Of course, not all attackers retreat quietly and you should be aware that the danger of violence always exists in these situations.

Things to Do

• When friends or acquaintances make a casual homophobic remark, correct their homophobia without using a hostile or confrontational tone. They may not be aware that what they said was offensive and just need to be informed. Using a hostile tone will create a negative atmosphere that could prevent them from getting the message. Ultimately the goal is to educate people about homophobia and how it affects you, not just to vent your anger.

• Be ready to debate the homophobes by having a basic knowledge of the standard propaganda and myths about gays and lesbians. (See pages 171–172.) A quick and knowledgeable response will reduce your opponents' confidence in their beliefs. All their arguments can be successfully challenged in a logical debate.

• Maintain control of your emotions when responding to a homophobic remark. Showing emotion or raising your voice can reduce the effectiveness of your response. Even if the opponent becomes emotional, you should stay calm, cool, and always be more logical and reasonable than him or her.

• Avoid name-calling. It makes people angry and defiant, thus unreachable. Instead of saying, "You're a homophobe," it is best to say, "That was a homophobic remark." With this approach you will find that the person becomes more responsive and you have a better chance of getting them to listen.

• Report it! If a stranger or someone you know threatens you with violence, report the incident to the anti-violence project and the local police. Many gays and lesbians have been physically assaulted by neighbors who had previously threatened violence.

17
Discuss Homophobia with Heterosexuals

BACKGROUND

The prevalence of homophobia has many consequences for gays and lesbians. Discrimination forces them to live as second-class citizens. Stigmatization excludes them from the mainstream and compels many to move from hostile rural environments to urban centers with large gay and lesbian populations like New York, San Francisco, Seattle, Atlanta, and Los Angeles. The danger of living in large gay and lesbian communities is that it can separate gays and lesbians from heterosexuals. While there are some who prefer to live their lives segregated from the mainstream and have little or no contact with heterosexuals, I believe the majority of gays and lesbians are open-minded about developing friendships with heterosexuals and maintaining congenial relationships with heterosexual family members.

Establishing and maintaining these friendships and relationships is not always easy. Openly gay and lesbian people have experiences, stemming from exclusion and stigmatization, that heterosexuals do not. Unless heterosexuals learn about these experiences and try to understand them, the barriers that divide cannot be erased. Therefore, for this reason, it is important for gays and lesbians to inform heterosexuals about their experiences with homophobia. While many of these experiences are obvious and easy to discuss and understand, others may seem unimportant or petty. It is these seemingly minor experiences with homophobia and its effects that often cause misunderstandings and offense. Examples of experiences that heterosexuals don't have to deal with:

• Knowing that holding hands with a companion in public puts you at risk.

• Strange reactions to ordinary scenes like a having a companion's photo on your desk. "Is that your brother?" "Is that your sister?" "No, it's my lover."

• When people believe and act as if heterosexual relationships are more valid than gay and lesbian relationships.

• Avoiding a social gathering because your companion was not invited.

• A friend turns to you in a restaurant and asks, "Why do you have to be so obvious?" putting him or herself in danger of becoming an ex-friend.

• Being unsure how strangers will react when they realize you are gay or lesbian.

• Strangers staring at you when they realize you are gay.

When strong, proud gays and lesbians encounter these types of experiences, they don't abandon their honest living and return to the closet. They keep striving to get heterosexuals to understand the difficulty that homophobia brings into everyday life.

Things to Do

• Determine which heterosexuals are capable of being good friends to gays and lesbians and are willing to understand your situation. (There are some hopeless cases.)

• Explain the issues and why gays and lesbians have to fight for civil rights and inclusion in mainstream society. While many heterosexuals support gay and lesbian rights, they often don't fully understand the issues and (unless they belong to another minority group) the consequences of being denied civil rights.

• Talk! Keep the lines of communication free and open and don't neglect the little incidents.

• If your heterosexual friends do or say something that offends you, tell them about it. Explain in a nonconfrontational tone how you feel and why.

• Tell your heterosexual friends that you are proud of your sexual orientation.

• Let your heterosexual friends know about the street battles. Women will relate easily to these battles. Tell about the insults and threats hurled at you.

• Show some understanding for heterosexuals who make mistakes with gay or lesbian friends. Remember, they don't have many of your experiences and therefore may not relate or have a different perspective. They rely on you for help in this area.

• Acknowledge and build on shared experiences and feelings—cultural events, work situations, family concerns, happiness, love, sadness, all the fundamentals of the human condition.

• Heterosexuals and gays and lesbians are different in a significant way. Celebrate the differences. Keep in mind that relationships and friendships with people from different backgrounds and with different experiences are enriching and expand one's universe.

18
Pursue Friendships with Gays and Lesbians

In this great country, founded on the principle that all people are created equal, we must learn to put aside what divides us and focus on what we share.
— PRESIDENT BILL CLINTON

BACKGROUND

Almost half of Americans say that they personally don't know someone who is gay or lesbian. Given that 10 percent of the entire population is gay or lesbian, this statistic reveals that many of these people have met gays or lesbians but they just don't know it. For this reason I encourage gays and lesbians to come out, and it is for this reason I now call on heterosexuals to do your part in breaking down the barriers between the two groups. Some heterosexuals who are ordinarily liberal and open-minded still hold misconceptions or oblique ideas about gays and lesbians. This can cause them unknowingly to commit homophobic acts, like voting against gay rights legislation or teaching their children that gays and lesbians are outcasts. These misconceptions can easily be dispelled by getting to know a gay man or a lesbian. When you become acquainted or friendly with an out gay or lesbian, you will learn that homophobic stereotypes have no basis, that they are individuals who share many of your concerns and feelings, and that their values and morals are not lesser or greater than yours. Above all, if you do not know an out gay or lesbian person, your views about homosexuality are probably abstract and surrounded by mystery. You can put a face on homosexuality and experience its reality by bringing gays and lesbians into your life.

You Should Know

• People least likely to know a homosexual: south central region (55 percent do not know any gays); those with less than a high school education (65 percent); those in small towns (54 percent).

• People most likely to know a homosexual: mountain states (64 percent); suburbanites (58 percent); college graduates (63 percent). (Source: *U.S. News & World Report*)

Things to Do

• Open your mind to diversity. The first step to accepting gays and lesbians as friends or acquaintances is a resolve to be open-minded.

• If you have fears or concerns about interacting with gays and lesbians, contact Parents and Friends of Lesbians and Gays (PFLAG). Call or write to the Washington chapter for the chapter closest to you and attend a meeting.

• Reach out to the gay and lesbian community in your town or city. It's easy. Just look in the phone book under "gay and lesbian" and call for information about the community. You will be surprised by the number of gays and lesbians who live in your area.

• Be prepared for the possibility of a negative reaction from some heterosexuals in regard to your gay and lesbian friendships. Inform these people that you love your gay and lesbian friends and have benefited from their friendship.

- Network with other heterosexuals to become involved in the healing process between gays, lesbians, and heterosexuals.
- Behave toward gay and lesbian friends the same way you behave toward heterosexuals.
- Don't exclude your gay and lesbian friends from social events comprised of heterosexuals.
- Include gay couples in couples events. It is in this area that many heterosexuals unknowingly hurt the feelings of gay couples. Some heterosexuals have an underlying belief that their relationships are more concrete or important than gay or lesbian relationships. Thus gays and lesbians often tell me about their disappointment and hurt when they are invited to an event like a wedding and their companion is not.
- If a gay or lesbian friend tells you that they are offended over something you said or did, listen without becoming defensive and assure them that you will think about what they said.
- If your gay or lesbian friend is going through a relationship breakup, show the same compassion for them as you would for a heterosexual friend. That pain is the same for everyone.
- Don't assume or imply that someone is homosexual because they have close relationships with gays and lesbians.
- Ask questions. Learn from your gay and lesbian friends about homosexuality and homophobia in your community.
- Be honest. Tell your new gay and lesbian friends about your reservations and fears and your struggle to overcome them.
- As you include gays and lesbians in your life, observe the changes in your attitudes toward and knowledge of homosexuality. You will find that the limitations you once inflicted on yourself and others have reduced and you will challenge traditional assumptions in other areas.

RESOURCES

McDonald, Helen B., and Audrey I. Steinhorn. "What Do You Mean You Are Not Heterosexual?" In *Understanding Homosexuality*. New York: Crossroad, 1993.

Thompson, Cooper. "On Being Heterosexual in a Homophobic World." In *Homophobia: How We All Pay the Price*. Warren J. Blumenfeld, ed. Boston: Beacon Press, 1992.

19
Learn What Your Children Learn About Gays and Lesbians

. . . Never, ever pass this injustice on to another generation.

—DAVID MIXNER

BACKGROUND

People are not born homophobic; they learn to be homophobic from others. This negative learning experience begins when a child is very young and it continues on through the process of socialization into adulthood. In order to decrease and eventually eliminate this attitude from society, we must teach children that homophobia, like all forms of bigotry, is wrong.

The task of preventing children from becoming homophobic or reeducating homophobic children begins in the home, where you have total control over what to teach, and continues later in the school environment. Don't throw up your hands and say, as one parent did, "What's the use, they will learn it in school anyway." There are two good reasons why you should avoid this defeatist thinking. First, even if children hear homophobic remarks at school you have the power to undo some of this damage. Second, you are not powerless over what children learn in school. You can get involved with the school boards;

you can find out how teachers view gays and lesbians by asking questions and you can then object if you hear something that is offensive.

Even people without children have a right to know what children are learning in the public schools. It is your responsibility as a taxpayer to ensure that your money is not being used to teach fear and hatred of gays and lesbians. As a citizen you have a right to attend community meetings and voice your opinions and concerns, and you have the voting power to elect responsible, nonhomophobic, open-minded school board members. Also, you can encourage family, friends, and coworkers with children to get involved with this issue.

You Should Know

• Children with poor self-esteem tend to be more prejudiced; those with higher self-esteem are more open-minded.

• In 1993, the New York City Board of Education attempted to introduce the Rainbow Curriculum, which promotes tolerance, including homosexuality, into the school system; the religious right and other antigay and lesbian forces mounted a successful campaign against the curriculum.

Things to Do

• Write to Alyson Publications requesting a catalogue of the children's books they have published. This gay- and lesbian-owned company publishes books for children ranging in age from two to twelve. Their titles include *Families*, *Heather Has Two Mommies*, *How Would You Feel If Your Dad Was Gay?*, and *The Generous Jefferson Bartleby Jones*.

• Ask your local library to stock these books and other material dealing with affirmative attitudes toward gays and lesbians.

• One way or another, your children are going to hear

about gays and lesbians; it is best for you to get to them first and clarify and explain things properly.

• Make sure that your children have firsthand experience with diversity. Encourage them to pursue friendships with children from different ethnic backgrounds.

• Join the PTA and discuss homophobia at meetings.

• Encourage your children to ask questions about gays and lesbians. Considering the prevalence of homophobic propaganda, children may become confused by the opposing ideas. Help them sort things out. Teach them about homophobia.

• If you are a teacher, invite people from gay and lesbian organizations to speak to your class. Contact a local gay and lesbian organization to get a recommended speaker and meet with the speaker before the event to review what will be discussed. Suggest to your school administrators that they have a "peer training" group visit your school. There are peer groups that go to high schools and discuss their experiences with homophobia.

• Attempt to undo negative peer training. Write the words *gay* and *lesbian* and ask your child to list the words they associate with gays and lesbians. This is a good way to find out what your children are learning.

• Teach your children that name-calling and harassment are wrong and unacceptable. Explain why: that it offends and injures them and others.

• Homophobic harassment in the classroom includes derogatory comments and slurs, violence, and harassing letters.

• Encourage children to talk about harassment.

• If your child is harassed in school, speak up. Talk to the teachers and administrators and let them know that you will not tolerate this persecution. Also, contact the American Federation of Teachers for more advice on how to deal with the situation.

• Encourage your children to keep a record of harassment. List the details, date, time, what happened, who did the harassing, and who witnessed it.

• Act promptly if you hear your child say something that is inappropriate.

• Observe your own behavior on a daily basis. Children are sensitive and observant.

• Attend school board meetings and pay particular attention to the curriculum. Listen to the language codes. "Family values" is a code term of the religious right and indicates that the user may be homophobic. These people will try to exclude from the curriculum any affirmative lessons on gays or lesbians. Don't believe the family values propaganda. Loving, caregiving, showing compassion, and teaching tolerance are the true family values.

• Demand that the school board provide sensitivity training for teachers, guidance counselors, and school administrators and that literature about sexual orientation be available in school libraries.

• If you know of an openly gay or lesbian teacher in your child's school, contact him or her. He or she will give you further advice on how to protect your children from homophobic influences.

• Ensure that your children watch affirmative gay and lesbian TV programs. There are not many. But CBS recently aired a Schoolbreak Special called *Other Mothers*, which was a sensitive portrait of a child with lesbian parents. If you missed this program, write to CBS, Entertainment Department, 51 West 52nd Street, New York, NY 10019, and request a rerun.

RESOURCES

Alyson Wonderland
Alyson Publications
Dept. H-80
40 Plympton St.
Boston, MA 02118
617-542-5679

American Federation of Teachers
National Gay and Lesbian Caucus
P.O. Box 19856
Cincinnati, OH 45219
Open Classroom: 513-242-2491

Gay and Lesbian Parents Coalition International
P.O. Box 50360
Washington, DC 20091
202-583-8029

Cohen, Susan and Daniel. *When Someone You Know Is Gay.* New York: M. Evans & Co., 1989. Written for heterosexual teenagers on the subject of homosexuality.
Willhoite, Michael. *Daddy's Roommate.* Boston: Alyson, 1990. (Rainbow Curriculum)

20
Encourage a Closeted Homosexual to Come Out

BACKGROUND

Many people, especially gays and lesbians, know someone who hides their sexual orientation. I once overheard a conversation between a heterosexual couple who were discussing a closeted gay friend. Despite their friend's attempts to hide his homosexuality, they knew he was gay, wondered why he was so secretive about it, and hoped he would eventually open up. Life is difficult for closeted gays and lesbians. They struggle endlessly to prevent others from discovering their secret, spending large amounts of time and energy dissembling and talking around subjects such as intimacy and romantic relationships. Often, all a closeted gay or lesbian needs is a catalyst, a sensitive, reassuring word from a friend or family member to help them dispel their fears and open up about their sexual orientation. Whether or not to intervene in these situations is a sensitive issue. Some people feel that it is no one's business and no one has a right to intervene. On the other hand, it is difficult to watch a friend or relative struggle with the hardships that arise from living a double life, especially when you know the quality of their life would improve if they came out. You have to decide for yourself what is the right thing to do. If you decide to approach your friend or relative, do so cautiously and sensitively and read my suggestions. *Don't* confuse this issue with outing. To *out* someone is to publicly or privately disclose the sexual orientation of a closeted person without the person's permission. I believe that outing is an invasion of privacy and can cause great harm, psychological and professional, to the closeted person. While it is vital for gays and lesbians to come out of the closet, encouragement, not outing, is the affirmative method to adopt.

EXAMPLES

Affirmative reasons why gays and lesbians should be open about their sexual orientation:

1. Their lives will be less complicated.

2. They will live fuller and healthier lives.

3. They will learn who their true friends are.

4. They will know what it's like to be loved for who they are.

5. They will establish a level of understanding with supportive friends and relatives that cannot be surpassed.

6. Their visibility will help reduce homophobia.

Things to Do

• Prepare for the discussion. Decide in advance how you will approach the issue and what you will say.

• Choose a comfortable, nonthreatening setting for the discussion: a restaurant, your home, or their home.

• Wait until the person is in a good mood.

- Make sure they realize that they have your complete and uncompromising support.
- Encourage them to resolve their internalized homophobia by seeking counseling with a gay and lesbian friendly therapist.
- Give your closeted friend an affirmative book dealing with coming out (see the list on page 38).
- Inform them about the many programs and support groups for gays and lesbians who want to come out of the closet.
- List reasons why they should come out of the closet.
- Mention the political aspects. For example, by being closeted, they contribute to the undercounting of the gay and lesbian population and therefore diminish its political power.
- Tell them that you are aware of the risks involved, but the benefits of living openly far outweigh the risks.
- Don't be discouraged if your discussion does not have an immediate impact. You will have made more of an impact than you realize. You have planted a seed, and, by doing so, have forced your friend to think about coming out. Accomplishing this is a good beginning.

21
Inform Homophobes That AIDS Is Not a Gay Disease

*Until people fully understand that we are all in this to-
gether—homosexual and heterosexual alike—and that we all
have the same rights, privileges, and responsibilities to one
another, we can never hope to beat this insidious disease. We
are talking about humanity here—not sexual preference.*
——ELIZABETH TAYLOR, ACTRESS/AIDS ACTIVIST

BACKGROUND

When acquired immune deficiency syndrome (AIDS) first sur-
faced in the United States it primarily afflicted gay men. As a result, this fatal disease became associated with homosexuality.
Because AIDS is sexually transmitted and many people view homosexuality and lesbianism in terms of sexual activity, gays and
lesbians, an already stigmatized minority, became further stigmatized. At first, before scientists discovered facts about the disease, there was widespread fear and panic: many people with
AIDS were shunned by friends and family, fired from their jobs,
denied medical treatment and basic civil rights. Yet, even
though scientists have determined that AIDS cannot be transmitted through casual contact, this form of discrimination continues. It is evident then that AIDS and HIV discrimination
arises not from fear of contacting the disease, but from homophobia. AIDS has become a potent weapon of the religious right

and other homophobes to justify discrimination against and to increase hatred and fear of gays and lesbians.

The notion that AIDS is a punishment for homosexuality is held not only by religious fanatics and extreme homophobes. I have heard people who seemed to be liberal refer to the "innocent victims" of AIDS. This implies that there are "guilty victims." Why is it that when heterosexuals like Ryan White, Arthur Ashe, and Kimberly Bergalis died from AIDS their plight received extensive mass media attention and generated much sympathy yet when renowned gay men die their deaths are acknowledged briefly by the mainstream media and they are quickly forgotten? This is homophobia in action. We must fight against this double standard and assert that *all* people inflicted with AIDS are innocent victims.

You Should Know

• In most parts of the world AIDS is a heterosexual disease. Heterosexual transmission of HIV is responsible for the alarmingly high rate of AIDS in Indonesia, Thailand, the Philippines, Uganda, Zambia, Rwanda, Malawi, Zaire, Haiti, India, and other nations.

• The World Health Organization estimates that by the year 2000, 40 million people will be infected with HIV.

Things to Do

• Challenge those who imply that AIDS and homosexuality are synonymous. Inform them that AIDS is a human disease and that there are large numbers of heterosexuals with AIDS, especially in Third World countries.

• Report all instances of HIV or AIDS discrimination to your local chapter of ACT UP and to the ACLU AIDS Project.

• Bring legal action against those who discriminate. The rights of people with AIDS and HIV are covered by laws protecting people with disabilities. Use these laws to put the discriminators on notice.

• Be wary of insurance companies. In an effort to screen out people with HIV and AIDS, they often openly discriminate against single men. Scrutinize all questionnaires from these companies. Look for questions geared toward unmarried men.

• Stay alive. Everyone—gays, lesbians, and heterosexuals—should practice safe sex. For information on safe sex, contact the national AIDS hotline and GMHC.

• Participate in demonstrations sponsored by ACT UP and other groups fighting AIDS and discrimination against gays and lesbians.

• Participate in AIDS walks, benefits, and other fund-raising events.

• Give your financial support to AIDS organizations.

• Subscribe to POZ magazine.

RESOURCES

ACT UP/Golden Gate
509 Castro St. #93
San Francisco, CA 94114
415-252-9200
fax: 415-252-9277

ACT UP/NEW YORK
135 West 29th St.
New York, NY 10001
212-564-2437
fax: 212-594-5441

American Civil Liberties Union
AIDS Project
132 West 43rd St.
New York, NY 10036
212-944-9800 ext. 545

Gay Men's Health Crisis (GMHC)
129 West 20th St.
New York, NY 10011
212-807-6664
hotline: 212-807-6655

God's Love We Deliver (provides hot meals for homebound people with AIDS)
895 Amsterdam Ave.
New York, NY 10025
212-865-4900

Names Project AIDS Memorial Quilt
Workshop and Education Center
1613 K St. NW
Washington, DC 20006
202-29-NAMES

National AIDS Hotline (24 hours a day)
800-342-AIDS

POZ Magazine
P. O. Box 1279
Old Chelsea Station
New York, NY 10113
800-883-2163
fax: 212-675-8505

22
Challenge Homophobic Talk Show Hosts

I say to those of you of the leftist, militant, homosexual crowd: take it somewhere else.

—RUSH LIMBAUGH

BACKGROUND

Radio talk shows hosted by mean-spirited and ignorant people have gained enormous popularity over the past ten years. On radio alone there are 800 talk stations around the country, and television talk shows are cropping up regularly, especially on cable. The format for talk shows varies little from show to show. The host begins with a monologue or diatribe that focuses on political and social issues in the news, announces the phone and fax numbers, and encourages the listeners to call in with their opinion and response. Unfortunately, the vast majority of radio talk shows, hosts, and listeners are conservative and reactionary, and needless to say, issues that involve gay and lesbian rights are treated harshly. In this medium dominated mostly by white males who in order to have high ratings and stay on the air must compete fiercely for listeners, homophobia dominates. Right-wing, cynical talk show hosts and their producers know how profitable it is to appeal to the basest aspects of human nature and thus busy themselves pandering to homophobic callers and spreading homophobia to millions of listeners. A friend of mine recently drove across the United States and listened to AM radio along the way. He told of his shock and dismay over the constant sexist and extreme homophobic statements that went unchallenged on talk radio. The callers, he observed, seemed to use the radio as a means of venting their anger or frustration with their lives—and, as usual, exempted themselves from taking responsibility and placed the onus for the problems in society on others.

While you may feel that you have better things to do than call talk shows, if you remain just a passive listener your ideas will go unheard and you will be relinquishing the airwaves to homophobes. As a medium, radio has great power to influence the opinions of millions of people. Politicians know this, and as elected officials and lawmakers, they take seriously what the hosts and callers say about them and their stand on the issues. It is up to you to let the hosts, the politicians, and your fellow listeners know that millions of people out there support gay and lesbian rights and are offended by homophobia on the airwaves. There are other reasons why you should challenge the homophobic views expressed on talk radio:

1. Your participation will reduce homophobia on talk radio.

2. Your participation will help create diversity on talk radio, which in the long run will elevate its cerebral value and change the dominant tone from confusion and anger to reason and understanding.

3. An effective challenge of the host's homophobic opinions will prompt some listeners to question what they hear.

4. Let Rush Limbaugh and his followers know that you do *not* intend to take it elsewhere, that you belong and are here to stay.

You Should Know

• Despite the prevalence of homophobic talk shows, there are progressive radio stations owned by organizations such as Pacifica and PBS that deal fairly and rationally with gay and lesbian rights issues. Pacifica's New York station (WBAI) airs talk shows hosted by gays and lesbians and gives substantial air time to the issues. These stations deserve your listenership and support during their fund-raising drives. Also, mainstream stations usually have token liberal hosts who get the worst time slots because they are ineffective and weak. They sometimes make a feeble attempt to combat and dissolve their listeners' homophobia, but do not have the facts or the determination necessary to succeed and are not above demonstrating mild homophobia of their own.

• The overwhelming majority of talk show listeners play a passive role and never call or participate in the discussion.

• Two of the most homophobic members of congress, Senator Jesse Helms (R-NC) and Representative Robert Dornan (R-CA), are former radio personalities.

• In 1994, nine talk radio hosts declared their candidacy for political office, believing their listeners to be their constituents.

• Among the most homophobic talk show hosts are Rush Limbaugh (nationally syndicated) and Bob Grant (WABC), who on the air often refer to gays and lesbian as perverts.

Things to Do

• Don't be afraid to call and express your opinions. There are two conflicting views on how to handle hate talk shows. Some people believe that it is best to ignore these shows because responding only gives them legitimacy and listener support, which is what they need to survive. Other people (me included) believe that these talk shows will survive with or without gay and lesbian input and it is important not to allow the homophobes to control the airwaves.

- Make a commitment to call at least one talk show a week.
- When you decide to call, make sure that you have facts to back up your argument.
- Maintain a calm tone of voice. Suppress the impulse to yell a string of abuses. If you become abusive, you will be playing into the hands of the hosts. They thrive on this kind of reaction. Use logic and coherent language. It's not difficult to win a debate with these guys because their opinions are grounded in bigotry, not fact.
- When the host realizes that you have the upper hand, he may attempt to quiet you by raising his voice and reciting a litany of stereotypical statements. Don't let this discourage you from calling again.
- Encourage others to call.
- Organize a phone zap with your friends. Choose a host who is overtly homophobic and call continuously.

23
Respond to Homophobia in Movies and on TV

As expressed on screen, America was a dream that had no room for homosexuals . . . and when the fact of our existence became unavoidable, we were reflected, on screen and off, as dirty secrets.

—VITO RUSSO, FILM HISTORIAN

BACKGROUND

Until recently the movie and television industries have either ignored the existence of gays and lesbians or have portrayed them in the usual grim, stereotypical fashion. In 1930 Hollywood moguls decided that self-censorship was the best way to protect the movie industry from outside censorship. They created the Motion Picture Production Code, which regulated the so-called morals of the industry until the 1960s. The code specifically forbade depictions of homosexuality (institutional homophobia) unless these depictions conformed to the perceptions held by homophobic people, namely, the homosexuality was unnatural and shameful. When gay and lesbian characters appeared on screen, either they had severe psychological problems or were suicidal, predators, or just basically miserable. Foreign films, such as *Madchen in Uniform*, that presented multidimensional and human portraits of gay and lesbian lives were banned or edited.

The treatment of homosexual subject matter on television

parallels that of the movie industry: there was nothing or there were deeply disturbed gay men and murderous lesbians. This mix of invisibility and negative stereotyping has harmed many people, gays and lesbians in particular, by reinforcing homophobia in America.

It was only in response to pressure brought on them by dedicated gay and lesbian activists that these industries began to hesitate before portraying negative stereotypes and attempted to diversify their images. Now there is a noticeable change in the way movies and television deal with homosexuality. It is not unusual to find gay and lesbian characters portrayed as normal people experiencing the same everyday conflicts, happiness, and sadness as their heterosexual counterparts. Gay and lesbian characters appear regularly on *Roseanne*, *L.A. Law*, and *Melrose Place*. Recent movies, including *Philadelphia*, *The Wedding Banquet*, *Threesome*, and *Serving in Silence: The Margarethe Cammermeyer Story* presented innovative depictions of gay and lesbian experience.

Despite this success, gay and lesbian rights activists still have to battle homophobia in movies and on television. *The Silence of the Lambs* and *Basic Instinct*, both made within the past three years and both huge box office hits, depicted stereotypical gay and lesbian characters. Also, homophobic programming still exists on TV: the sitcom *Martin* on the Fox Network relies heavily on homophobic humor.

Whether the way the media portrays gays and lesbians may make you grateful or annoyed, it is important to respond and let the networks know that you are tracking homophobia in the media.

Things to Do

- When you see homophobia in a movie, find out who the

producers and distributors are. You can find this information in newspaper ads for the movie.

• Write a letter to the producers and distributors complaining about the movie's homophobia.

• Discuss your observations with others. If they agree with you, encourage them to write also.

• When you see a positive depiction of the gay and lesbian experience in a movie, write to the producers and inform them of your support.

• When a TV network presents a program that depicts gays and lesbians in a positive way, call or write to the network informing them of your support. TV networks are constantly under pressure from antigay and lesbian forces not to depict the gay and lesbian experience. Your call or letter will counteract this negative pressure.

• Pay attention to which corporations support positive gay and lesbian programming with advertising and buy their products.

• When you see a homophobic program on TV, record the program and be sure to include the advertisements. It is important to know which corporations support homophobia with advertising.

• Call or write to the network responsible for homophobic programming and express your concern and disappointment that they are promoting homophobia.

• Call or write to networks that succumb to pressure from antigay and lesbian forces. For example, the Fox network caved in to pressure from the religious right and censored a kiss between the two gay characters on *Melrose Place*. Let Fox feel some pressure from the other side of the issue.

• Watch gay and lesbian programming on cable and PBS. PBS presents a regularly scheduled gay and lesbian series called *In The Life*. The schedule varies from station to station, so call 800-627-ONTV to find out when it's on in your area.

• Join the Gay and Lesbian Alliance Against Defamation (GLAAD) and become involved.

• Report positive and negative depictions of the gay and lesbian experience in the media to GLAAD and to media columnists of the gay and lesbian publications *Out*, *Genre*, and *The Advocate* (see pages 119–120).

• When you become a member of GLAAD you will receive their newsletter. In it they provide phone numbers and addresses of the organizations that need either to be thanked or reprimanded. Be sure to follow GLAAD's advice and take the actions they recommend.

RESOURCES

Fox Network, Inc.
Viewer Services
205 East 67th St.
New York, NY 10021
212-452-3600

National headquarters of the Gay and Lesbian Alliance Against Defamation

GLAAD
150 West 26th St., #503
New York, NY 10001
212-807-1700
fax: 212-807-1806

GLAAD
8455 Beverly Blvd., #305
Los Angeles, CA 90048
213-658-6775
fax: 213-658-6776

Field offices include:

GLAAD/Boston
338 Newbury St.
Boston, MA 02115
617-492-4639

GLAAD/SF/Bay Area
514 Castro St., #B
San Francisco, CA 94114-2512
415-861-2244
fax: 415-861-4893

For further listings of GLAAD field offices, call or write to:
Donna Red Wing
1130 SW Morrison, Suite 607
Portland, OR 97205
503-224-5285
fax: 503-224-5480

In The Life Media, Inc. (gay and lesbian network)
30 West 26th St.
New York, NY 10010
800-301-6012

24
Be Aware of Exploitation of Gays and Lesbians

Am I not the greatest friend of the lesbian community?
—HOWARD STERN

BACKGROUND

Gays and lesbians belong to a marginal group in society and as such are vulnerable to all types of abuses, including exploitation. Many instances occur where straight individuals or organizations exploit homosexuality and lesbianism for their own profit. The most famous and obvious exploiter of all is Howard Stern, who on radio, TV, and in his book uses lesbianism to titillate his straight male audience. "Lesbians bring home the ratings," Stern maintains as he parades these so-called lesbians before the nation in a demeaning, freak show atmosphere. Stern's perception of lesbianism is a straight man's fantasy and appeals only to straight men. It has nothing to do with lesbianism. Lesbians, in general, are repelled by the fact that many straight men get off on lesbian sexuality and are careful not to allow them this satisfaction. Perhaps some of the women who appear on Stern's show are actually lesbian, but we all know that some people would do anything, even sell out their own community, for attention and money. In addition, while Stern claims to love lesbians (after all, they bring home the ratings), he makes disparaging remarks about homosexuality and often calls gay men "homos."

Things to Do

• Be aware that exploitation of gays and lesbians exists and do everything possible not to support it.

• When you witness exploitation, bring it to the attention of other gays and lesbians and encourage them not to support it.

• Don't listen to the Howard Stern program and don't participate in his lesbian freak shows. Find another way to make a buck.

• Inform the exploiters that you are aware of their exploitation.

• Don't confuse exploitation with visibility. Just because gays and lesbians have been invisible in the media for so long does not mean that they should accept any type of exposure. Some forms of exposure are questionable. On the surface it may appear to be valid but with a closer look you will discover that it promotes homophobia.

25
Understand Institutional Homophobia and Its Impact

*My straight characters never seemed to cause the studio
executives a moment's pause, but I was told repeatedly that
the gay ones could never be shown on television in romantic
situations.*

—ARMISTEAD MAUPIN

BACKGROUND

Institutional homophobia occurs when organizations, businesses, churches, and government discriminate on the basis of sexual orientation. Contrary to the rhetoric of some conservatives, institutional discrimination against gays and lesbians is widespread. Organizations and institutions enact laws, codes, decrees, or policies to enforce homophobic discrimination. Unfortunately, there are plenty of examples: The Catholic Church and the Southern Baptist Church proclaim homosexual acts to be sinful and direct their clergy to preach against homosexuality. The Boy Scouts of America has a national policy that bars membership to gays and lesbians. And, of course, the Pentagon legally bans openly gay and lesbian individuals from serving in the military. In 1991, Cracker Barrel Old Country Store, Inc. enacted an antigay and lesbian policy that stated the company would only hire heterosexuals. As a result, at least eleven employees were fired because they were gay. The company's shareholders objected, demanding that Cracker Barrel end its antigay stance and enact a nondiscrimination rule. Cracker Barrel dropped the policy but refused to adopt a nondiscrimination rule. In 1993, a group of shareholders filed a lawsuit demanding the right to vote on an antibias policy during its annual shareholders meeting. On October 15, 1993, Judge Kimba Wood ruled that the shareholders have a right to vote on this policy. The shareholders who brought the lawsuit still don't have enough votes to get the policy enacted.

Despite these and other instances of discrimination based on sexual orientation, over the last twenty years the gay and lesbian civil rights movement has achieved great success fighting institutional homophobia. Many political jurisdictions across the country have enacted gay rights legislation, making it illegal to discriminate on the basis of sexual orientation.

While the momentum seems to be going in the right direction, there still is a long way to go before gays and lesbians are protected from discrimination.

Examples of How Institutional Homophobia is Harmful

- It leads to discrimination and exclusion and deprives gays and lesbians of basic civil rights, including housing, employment, and police protection.
- It sends a message to society that gays and lesbians are second-class citizens.
- Some gays and lesbians begin to *feel* like second-class citizens and their self-esteem becomes eroded.
- To avoid discrimination, many gays and lesbians hide their sexual orientation and live double lives.
- The courts often deny gay and lesbian parents custody of their children.
- Through the use of sodomy laws (twenty-five states still

have them), government denies gay men the right to sexual expression.

• It is antidemocratic and violates this country's commitment to equality and individual liberty.

Things to Do

• Learn more about institutional homophobia and how it affects you and others.

• Understand that this discrimination is often subtle or obscured by the institution, yet your instincts tell you about it. For example, a friend of mine who is a slightly effeminate gay man went for a job interview at a major airline. The first interview went very well and the interviewer determined that he was qualified for the job. The second interview, which was supposed to be a formality, was conducted by a different person and was a disaster. My friend claimed that the interviewer looked at him with disdain and told him he was unqualified. While there is no concrete evidence here of discrimination, my friend is adamant that he felt discriminated against. If you feel it, then it is probably real.

• List occasions when you believe you were discriminated against by an organization or institution. Include where the incident occurred, your age, and how you responded.

• For each item listed discover how it impacted on your life and well-being.

• Write a letter to each organization or institution, addressed to the public relations department, informing them how they violated your rights and that you intend to prevent such discrimination in the future.

• Inform heterosexual friends and family members about institutional homophobia and your experiences with it.

• Make a commitment to eliminate institutional homophobia.

• Volunteer your time and give financial support to organizations working for gay and lesbian rights legislation and encourage your friends to do the same.

• Stay positive! Remind yourself of the many positive changes that have already occurred and, with dedication and hard work, how many more will be accomplished in the future.

RESOURCES

Human Rights Campaign Fund
P.O. Box 1396
Washington, DC 20013
202-628-4160
fax: 202-347-5323

National Gay and Lesbian Task Force
2320 17th St. NW
Washington, DC 20009
202-332-6483
fax: 202-332-0207

Mohr, Richard, D. *A More Perfect Union: Why Straight Americans Must Stand Up for Gay Rights.* New York: Farrar Straus & Giroux, 1994.

Nava, Michael, and Robert Dawidoff. *Created Equal: Why Gay Rights Matters to America.* New York: St. Martin's Press, 1994.

26
Know Your Rights

It is revolting to have no better reason for a rule of law than that . . . it was laid down in the time of Henry IV. It is still more revolting if the grounds upon which it was laid down have vanished long since.
> —FORMER SUPREME COURT JUSTICE
> HARRY BLACKMUN ON SODOMY LAWS

A Federal judge has declared the military's ban on gay men and lesbians to be unconstitutional.
> —THE NEW YORK TIMES 9/3/93

A Colorado initiative that outlawed gay rights laws was declared unconstitutional today.
> —THE WASHINGTON POST 12/15/93

BACKGROUND

There is overwhelming evidence to demonstrate that gays and lesbians are routinely discriminated against in employment, housing, the military, family matters, AIDS and HIV infection, and education. A lesbian mother loses custody of her son; a gay employee at Cracker Barrel is fired; a gay officer is discharged from the navy. At times, the list of rights violations against gays and lesbians seems overwhelming. Today, as more and more gays and lesbians are unwilling to hide their sexual orientation and tolerate discrimination, the struggle for civil rights is taking place not only on the political front, but also in the courts. These challenges have put the issue of gay and lesbian rights in the national spotlight, producing significant victories that have given hope and courage to everyone concerned about justice.

A federal law banning discrimination would provide the best protection for gays and lesbians. The Human Rights Campaign Fund and the National Gay and Lesbian Task Force are currently lobbying for a federal civil rights law. In 1994, a pared-down version of the civil rights bill was introduced in Congress. It is called the Employee Nondiscrimination Act and has 31 cosponsors in the Senate and 137 cosponsors in the House. The gay lobbyists are confident that this legislation will be enacted. Also, gays and lesbians may have recourse on the state and local level, where, especially in major metropolitan areas, there are statutes, ordinances, and executive orders making it unlawful to discriminate on the basis of sexual orientation.

It is important for you to know if the district, city, or state in which you live has laws banning discrimination based on sexual orientation. To find out what the laws are in your jurisdiction, contact a civil rights lawyer or call or write to the American Civil Liberties Union. In addition, there are many things you can do to protect yourself in civil areas of the law. The ACLU publishes a series of handbooks dealing with citizens' rights, including a guide called *The Rights of Lesbians and Gay Men*; the information provided is current and basic. Should you discover that your rights have been violated and you have legal recourse, it is in your best interest, and the best interest of all gays and lesbians, that you take action against the offenders.

Things to Do

• Buy the ACLU handbook and the legal guides listed below. In them you will find important information about how to protect your rights in all areas of the laws.

• Because no state recognizes gay and lesbian marriage, partners of gays and lesbians are not considered to be next of kin; therefore couples should plan ahead and draft legal documents like wills and living wills giving their partners the right to inherit, if that's the choice, and a durable power of attorney designating that the gay or lesbian partner has the power to make medical and financial decisions in case of illness or accident. Without these documents the state and family members can deny gays and lesbians the right to act on behalf of their partners.

- All gays and lesbians, whether they are single or in relationships, should have wills and living wills.

- You are not legally required to use a lawyer to draft legal documents, but in order to ensure that legal documents are drafted correctly, you should consult a lawyer.

- Use a lawyer who is familiar with the specific needs of gays and lesbians. Contact Lambda for a recommendation.

- Gay and lesbian parents should have parenting agreements that cover issues such as defining the relationship between the nonbiological parent and the children, or adoption agreements, financial responsibilities involved in child rearing, and custody arrangements in case the relationship terminates.

- Report violations of your civil rights to ACLU and Lambda.

- Find out if your state has a sodomy law and work with civil rights groups to have it repealed.

- When renting an apartment, gay and lesbian couples should include both partners' names on the lease.

- Consult a lawyer if faced with discrimination or threatened with eviction.

- Know the fundamentals: read the Bill of Rights.

- Be affirmative! Don't allow any group or individual to teat you like a second-class citizen.

- Save all documents relating to employment, housing, insurance policies, health care, adoptions, and legal actions.

• Take advantage of the many organizations that provide legal assistance.

• Financially support nonprofit groups like Lambda Legal Defense, the ACLU, and the National Center for Lesbian Rights that work to protect gay and lesbian rights.

RESOURCES

American Civil Liberties Union
(see page 91)

Center for Constitutional Rights
666 Broadway
New York, NY 10012
212-614-6464

Gay and Lesbian Advocates and Defenders
P.O. Box 218
Boston, MA 02112
617-426-1350

Lambda Legal Defense and Education Fund, Inc.
666 Broadway
New York, NY 10012
212-995-8585
fax: 212-995-2306

606 South Olive St., Suite 580
Los Angeles, CA 90036
213-937-2728
fax: 213-937-0610

National Center for Lesbian Rights
1663 Mission St.
San Francisco, CA 94103
415-392-6257

Curry, Hayden, Denis Clifford, and Robin Leonard. *A Legal Guide for Lesbians & Gay Couples*. Berkeley: Nolo Press, 1993.

Hunter, Nan, Sherryl E. Michaelson, and Thomas B. Stoddard. *The Rights of Lesbians and Gay Men*. Carbondale, IL: Southern Illinois University Press, ACLU handbook, 3rd ed., 1992.

Life Planning: Legal Documents & Protection for Lesbians & Gay Men. New York: Lambda Legal Defense and Education Fund booklet, 1992.

27
Attend Demonstrations

The only thing necessary for the triumph of evil is for good men [and women] to do nothing.

—EDMUND BURKE

BACKGROUND

The founders of the United States knew how important it is for citizens of a democracy to have the right to express dissent. Therefore, in the First Amendment to the Constitution, they ensured "the right of the people peaceably to assemble, and to petition the Government for a redress of grievances." Throughout the history of this country reformers have used this basic right as a weapon in the fight against injustice. Americans who fought for female suffrage and African-American civil rights relied on protest demonstrations, large and small, as an effective method of informing the government of their discontent and bringing public attention to their cause. Across the country gay and lesbian rights organizations hold demonstrations to protest discrimination based on sexual orientation, antigay and lesbian violence, and a variety of other rights issues.

Demonstrations differ in tone depending on the issue involved and the mood of the demonstrators. Candlelight and prayer vigils are silent but powerful statements of protest. Gay and lesbian activists sometimes use them for issues concerning AIDS or to memorialize victims of hate crimes. Other demonstrations are loud rallies where the demonstrators express their anger and their determination to overcome injustice by chanting slogans and making speeches. Whatever the tone of the demonstration the key to whether or not it attracts productive attention to the cause is that it be nonviolent. It is the responsibility of the demonstrators and organizers to maintain control over themselves and not allow spectators or even the police to provoke a situation that will be counterproductive, repelling more people from the issue than it attracts.

For those who are brave and truly devoted there is a type of demonstration known as nonviolent civil disobedience. In most forms of nonviolent civil disobedience the demonstrators decide before the demonstration to commit a misdemeanor like sitting down in the road or entering a restricted area, thereby subject themselves to arrest. These demonstrators allow the police to make the arrest in a controlled and orderly fashion. Nonviolent civil disobedience is extremely effective in that it always receives media attention. In the spring of 1994, a group of high-ranking politicians took part in a nonviolent civil disobedience in Washington, DC, to protest the Clinton administration's policy concerning Haiti. Within days the administration announced a change in its Haitian policy. Before engaging in this form of protest, know the consequences of being arrested, have a bail source ready, and expect eventually to pay a fine. Groups that sponsor nonviolent civil disobedience usually hold meetings prior to the event and inform the participants of the consequences of being arrested and show them how to behave during the arrest to prevent any disturbance.

You Should Know

• The first gay and lesbian rights demonstration was held in New York City in 1963. Demonstrators picketed the draft induction center, protesting the military's discrimination against gays and lesbians.

• In 1965, gay and lesbian activists picketed the White House for the first time. They protested antigay and lesbian employment policies by the federal government. This demonstration received extensive coverage in the mainstream media.

Things to Do

• Don't be afraid to attend demonstrations. They are legal and you can't get into trouble unless you provoke it by behaving in a counterproductive manner. It is your right and duty as a citizen to raise your voice in public against homophobia.

• Keep abreast of the issues and informed about demonstrations. The best way to stay informed is to join a political organization fighting for gay and lesbian rights and attend meetings. Direct action groups include NGLTF, GLAAD, Queer Nation, Lesbian Avengers, and Gay and Lesbian Americans.

• Make a commitment to participate in a demonstration and mark it in your calendar.

• Know the exact reasons for and goals of the demonstration. In most cases, gay and lesbian organizations only call for demonstrations when they need to apply pressure and after negotiations with the offending group have failed.

• Contribute visually by making a placard with your message and display it.

• Add your name to a phone tree. Gay and lesbian groups use phone trees to inform their members of demonstrations.

• Encourage family members and friends to join the demonstration.

• Know the groups involved and avoid any outside agitators. Sometimes individuals or organizations unaffiliated with the cause and with the other agendas attend demonstrations to agitate and incite violence.

- Inform the organizers if you suspect someone of being a provocateur.
- Organize your own demonstration. If you become aware of a homophobic incident or are just fed up with homophobia in your town or county, take the initiative by bringing it to the attention of gay and lesbian rights groups and organize protest activities. Grassroots organizing is vital for the success of any rights movement.
- Before organizing a demonstration, contact the American Civil Liberties Union to learn the procedure.
- Evaluate the outcome of the demonstration. Every demonstration achieves something whether it is bringing public attention to the cause or prompting politicians to take action. Listing the accomplishments will provide encouragement and motivation for future protests.
- Evaluate what you got out of it.
- Before attending the demonstration, be prepared for the possibility of media presence. You should be ready to speak to the press about the demonstration and have the facts of the situation ready. Your statement should be brief, to the point, and delivered articulately and in a calm and sane tone.
- Prior to the demonstration call your local newspapers and TV stations to inform them of the protest.

RESOURCES

ACT UP
(see page 90)

Gay and Lesbian Americans (grassroots organizing)
Lesbian and Gay Community Services Center
208 West 13th St.
New York, NY 10003
212-978-7940

Lesbian Avengers
Lesbian and Gay Community Services Center
208 West 13th St.
New York, NY 10003
212-967-7711 ext. 3204

Queer Nation
Lesbian and Gay Community Services Center
208 West 13th St.
New York, NY 10003
212-260-6156

Mondros, Jacqueline B., and Scott M. Wilson. *Organizing for Power and Empowerment.* New York: Columbia University Press, 1994.

28
Subscribe to Gay and Lesbian Magazines

BACKGROUND

Gays and lesbians first began producing their own magazines and newspapers back in the forties and fifties to fill the void left by the mainstream press. At that time they knew that if they wanted to read unbiased and realistic reports about their lives they would have to create their own press. The gay and lesbian press became an important factor in the rights movement that followed. The magazines and newspapers that emerged served as a unifying force by providing information, functioning as a vehicle for expression, and presenting gay and lesbian perspectives on issues. At first, subscriptions were low, advertising was scarce, and publications struggled to survive on shoestring budgets. Yet, if one folded, a new publication often emerged to take its place.

As the gay and lesbian rights movement grew, subscriptions to publications rose, allowing them to grow, change, and become more polished. Today, there are even national magazines that are glossy and attract mainstream advertisers, and around the country there are local weekly newspapers in all major metropolitan areas serving the needs of gays, lesbians, and their supporters.

In order for magazines and newspapers to remain financially secure, advertising is essential. The ability to attract lucrative, mainstream advertising depends on the publication's circulation. Your subscription increases the circulation, which in turn provides advertisers with a concrete reason for investing in the gay and lesbian market. Some advertisers, such as Sony, Apple Computer, Virgin Airlines, Naya, and Miller Brewing Company, already recognize the importance of the gay market and have begun placing ads in gay and lesbian publications. It is up to gays, lesbians, and their supporters to continue this trend and subscribe to the publications that are a vital part of the civil rights movement.

You Should Know

• In June 1947, using the anagram Lisa Ben, a secretary for a Hollywood movie studio published the first lesbian magazine in the United States. It was called *Vice Versa* and Ms. Ben produced and distributed the magazine herself.

• In January 1953, *One* became the first gay men's magazine published in the United States. The U.S. Post office refused to allow *One* to be circulated through the mail, maintaining that articles about homosexuality were obscene. A lawsuit ensued and in 1958 the U.S. Supreme Court ruled in favor of *One*; this ruling become the first major victory in the courts for gay and lesbian rights.

Things to Do

• If you are on a limited income and cannot afford to subscribe to all the magazines, then be sure to include *The Advocate* in your choice. *The Advocate* provides the best political coverage and its biweekly publication allows the reader to keep up to date on the issues. Staying informed is critical in your fight against homophobia.

• You don't have to be gay or lesbian to subscribe. Encourage friends and relatives to subscribe. Heterosexuals will find that some of the issues covered extensively in the gay and lesbian press, such as civil rights, censorship, AIDS, and the Christian Coalition's agenda, concern everyone.

• Subscriptions make great gifts. Give them to friends and family for birthdays and holidays.

• Ask your local newsstand to stock gay and lesbian publications.

• Sometimes when magazine stores sell gay and lesbian magazines they keep them in the pornography section in the back. Check your neighborhood store and ask them not to stock gay and lesbian publications with pornography, unless, of course, they are pornographic.

• Don't neglect the local gay and lesbian newspapers. Buy one at every opportunity. They provide news from the local front, announcements for important events, and information about local businesses and politicians. They are important vehicles for grassroots organizing.

• You can find these national magazines and local newspapers at your gay and lesbian bookstore.

• Support businesses that advertise in gay and lesbian publications by buying their products.

• Renew your subscriptions as soon as they expire.

NATIONAL PUBLICATIONS

The Advocate (The National Gay & Lesbian Newsmagazine)
6922 Hollywood Blvd., 10th fl.
Los Angeles, CA 90028
1-800-827-0561

BLK (magazine for African-American gays and lesbians)
P.O. Box 83912
Los Angeles, CA 90083
310-410-0808

Deneuve (The Lesbian Magazine)
2336 Market St., #15
San Francisco, CA 94114
415-863-6538
fax: 415-863-1609

Genre (Gay men's magazine covering fashion, arts and entertainment, politics)
P.O. Box 25169
Anaheim, CA 92895
800-576-9933

Out (culture, media, politics, work, fashion, health)
110 Greene St.
New York, NY 10012
800-876-1199

10 Percent (politics, arts, and entertainment)
54 Mint St., #200
San Francisco, CA 94103
415-905-8590
fax: 415-227-0463

29
Write a Letter to the Editor

The pen is mightier than the sword.

BACKGROUND

The mainstream press began limited coverage of the gay and lesbian rights movement following the Stonewall Rebellion. During the past five years, however, as the movement has gained momentum and more gays and lesbians are coming out and becoming visible, mainstream coverage has increased considerably. Now all major newspapers and newsmagazines report on the political and social success and failures of the movement. Some, like *The New York Times*, cover the issues in editorials and op-ed pieces. As a result, the debate over gay and lesbian rights flourishes within the mainstream press. Supporters and homophobes alike have leaped into the fray, writing letters, editorials, and articles that millions of people around the country are reading.

You can join the debate over gay and lesbian rights by presenting your opinions in letters to the editors of newspapers and magazines. There are many reasons why you should become involved in this way, for example:

1. It is important that letters of support outnumber those of the opposition. When this occurs, editors and publishers will learn that the majority of readers support gay and lesbian rights and this in turn will affect the publication's attitude toward the issue.

2. Even if the editors choose not to print your letter, you will receive personal gratification from having taken meaningful action in the fight against homophobia and the psychological benefit of expressing your feelings.

3. Gays, lesbians, and their supporters are gratified and encouraged when they read letters in newspapers that challenge homophobia.

4. Because of the power and influence of the press, it is dangerous to allow homophobia in newspapers and magazines to go unchallenged.

You Should Know

There are some factors you need to consider when writing your letter:

• The letter should be short, three short paragraphs at the most.

• Refer directly to the article, editorial, or letter to which you are responding, specifying the date it appeared in the publication, its title, and author.

• The letter should be grammatically correct and written in standard English or Spanish.

• Get to the point quickly and do not diverge from the immediate subject.

• The tone should be rational. You are clarifying and explaining, not just venting anger.

• Contradict homophobic assumptions by using facts and appealing to common sense. Your goal should be to set the record straight.

Things to Do

- You will find the address to send your letter on the editorial page.
- Read other letters printed in the newspapers to get a feel for the standards that the editors require.
- Allow someone whose opinion you value to read your letter and critique its contents.
- Don't send a computer-formatted letter. While these types of letters are useful for mass mailings and fund-raising, they are generally boring, most people hate reading them, and you can be sure that it will not be printed.
- Encourage friends and other supporters to write letters.
- It may be difficult and too time-consuming for you to respond every time something comes up, but make a commitment to respond when something printed really disturbs you.
- Respond to letters written by homophobes. In the interest of healthy debate many publications print letters that challenge the letters they printed.
- Respond also to positive items, thanking the editor for running a positive story or editorial and agreeing with its content. Institutions that deal in an affirmative way with gay and lesbian rights endure great pressure and scrutiny from the homophobic forces. Acknowledge their courage and fair-mindedness.
- Don't be discouraged if your letter is not printed. Just keep on writing.

30
Sign Petitions and
Organize Petition Drives

BACKGROUND

Petition drives are a fundamental and effective form of direct action. A petition is a formal request to an organization or person in power asking redress for or correction of an existing situation that the petitioners deem to be unjust. The power of a petition exists primarily in its ability to represent an action taken by many people. It demonstrates the opinion of a group and indicates to the recipient that there is awareness, unity, and determination around the issue at hand. When it comes to politics and social reform, one cannot seriously doubt or dismiss the power and strength of numbers. Politicians depend on numbers for their election and if, for example, a politician discovers that he or she will lose hundreds of votes by opposing gay and lesbian rights legislation, he or she will be concerned. Business is also a numbers game. Without the patronage of many people, businesses cannot be profitable and will not survive.

Antigay and lesbian forces have successfully used petition drives as a means of influencing the public and people in power.

Organizations like the Oregon Citizens Alliance instituted grass-roots petition drives to add antigay and lesbian initiatives to the state and local ballots in 1993. The statewide initiative was narrowly defeated but the OCA reintroduced the initiative in 1994. The American Civil Liberties Union challenged the constitutionality of the initiative and won. But the OCA appealed the court decision and in September 1994 the court of appeals ruled in favor of the OCA, thereby putting the initiative on the ballot. The leaders of the Oregon Citizens Alliance were confident that this time the majority of voters would support the antigay and lesbian initiative. But they were wrong. The initiative (Measure 13) was defeated. This demonstrates that supporters of gay and lesbian rights, individuals, and organizations can win the hearts and minds of people. There are plenty of fair-minded people who are willing to listen and, after learning the facts, will do the right thing.

SAMPLE PETITION STATEMENT

We, the undersigned, are a group of concerned citizens who support the civil rights of gays and lesbians and deplore the discrimination they often experience in employment, housing, and child custody. While some districts within the state have amended their local nondiscrimination law to include sexual orientation, most gays and lesbians still lack the legal protection necessary to defend themselves from this discrimination. For this reason it is necessary to enact a *state* law that would provide gays and lesbians with the legal recourse essential for protection.

We strongly urge you to support the bill now before the state senate that would make discrimination against gays and lesbians illegal. You should know that the rights of gays and lesbians are as important to us as the rights of other citizens and we intend to keep this issue alive in our communities and on our minds when we go to the polls.

Respectfully yours,

Things to Do

• Identify the *targets* of the petitions. Sending a petition to politicians who have already publicly stated their position, whether it is pro or con, is futile. Your target in the political arena should be the undecided. Help them to make the right decision.

• Before sending a petition to a corporation or organization, find out who has the authority to make changes and target them. The person you want to reach is the one with whom the buck stops. Call the organization repeatedly until you have identified the person with the power to make a difference.

• Write your petition statement. It should be as brief as possible and you should demonstrate your determination and concerns in a polite and respectful tone. You catch more bees with honey than with vinegar. If necessary, don't be embarrassed to get help writing the statement.

• Remember, petitions do not have to have thousands or even hundreds of signatures. A petition with fifty signatures can be effective.

• Send a copy of your petition to more than one politician.

• Encourage people to sign, emphasizing the moral issue involved. Explain the issue clearly, describing the dangers to a society if injustice prevails.

• Ask everyone you know, including neighbors, friends, family, and coworkers, to sign.

• Go into areas with large gay and lesbian populations.

• Get others to collect signatures for your petition.

• Get a local gay and lesbian organization involved in your drive.

- Send copies of the petition to newspapers and perhaps you will get some free publicity.

- Never sign a petition unless you know exactly what it intends to achieve. Many people who signed petitions putting antigay and lesbian rights initiatives on the ballot were victimized by the homophobic propaganda and unaware that the initiative would deprive citizens of basic rights.

- A petition is merely a formal document and can be used in different ways to fight homophobia. It can be used as a newspaper ad. Often a group of concerned citizens and organizations join forces, pool their resources, and place these ads. For example, a recent ad campaign launched by GLAAD/NY and the Empire State Pride Agenda used a petition format to call public attention to facts about antigay and lesbian discrimination and the need for state legislation to make it illegal.

31
Join Gay and Lesbian Political Organizations

You don't convince other people to let you have more power. You build political power. That's how you win rights for yourself.

—SARAH SCHULMAN

BACKGROUND

The political power and influence of gay men and lesbians depends to a large degree on the strength and unity of gay and lesbian political organizations. Fortunately, over the past twenty-five years many organizations have been supported by the community and grown large and powerful both on the national and local levels. While each organization may focus on different issues or use different approaches to activism, they all share the same agenda, which is to maintain widespread visibility, fight injustice, and protect the rights of gays and lesbians. These organizations depend on their membership for survival and strength. A direct correlation exists between the success of an organization and the size of its membership. A large membership gives the group the financial resources necessary to employ a substantial and experienced staff, maintain state of the art offices, become involved in projects, and thus fight effectively against the religious right and lobby successfully in the political arena. In addition, the existence of large organizations demonstrate to the powers that be the dedication and strength of the gay and lesbian rights movement.

Given that gays and lesbians comprise 10 percent of the population and that most of them are concerned about the violation of their rights, membership in gay and lesbian organizations should be extremely high. Yet, although the membership of all the major organizations is growing steadily, the numbers are still not as impressive as they could be. This is where you come in. As a gay or lesbian person or a concerned heterosexual, you can contribute enormously to the movement, get involved, and keep informed of the latest issues by becoming a member of a national or local gay and lesbian rights organization.

Things to Do

• Contact an organization(s) you would want to be affiliated with and get membership information. Annual full membership dues for gay and lesbian organizations average around $40. But if you can afford to contribute more, then do; it is money well spent.

• Become actively involved in the organization by volunteering your time and donating office supplies or computer equipment. Don't limit yourself to a passive membership, contributing only financially.

• Circulate the organization's newsletter or bulletin among your friends and encourage them to join.

• Newsletters will give you updated information on gay and lesbian issues and often ask members to call or write letters concerning a particular issue. It is important for you to take the time to do this. The address and phone numbers are always included in the newsletters.

• Donate also to gay and lesbian community centers and volunteer your time.

• When your membership expires, renew it promptly.

MAJOR GAY AND LESBIAN ORGANIZATIONS

Gay and Lesbian Alliance Against Defamation was founded in 1985. Its focus is on fighting for fair, accurate, and inclusive representations of lesbian and gay lives, especially in the media. GLAAD has national offices in New York and Los Angeles, and chapters in most major cities.

Gay and Lesbian Americans was founded in 1994 by activist Michael Petrelis. This new national organization is a direct-action group that will focus on fighting the antigay forces throughout the country by using grassroots organizing. GLA will also do some lobby work for AIDS research funding and for passage of federal antidiscrimination protection on the basis of sexual orientation.

Gay and Lesbian Independent Democrats was founded in 1974 and is a progressive gay and lesbian Democratic club based in New York City.

Gay and Lesbian Victory Fund is based in Washington, DC, and its purpose is to support openly gay and lesbian candidates for office.

International Lesbian and Gay Association was founded in 1978 and is a worldwide network of grassroots organizations concerned with legal, social, cultural, and economic discrimination against gays and lesbians on a global level. ILGA was recognized by the United Nations as an international organization in 1993. But unfortunately, the United States delegation challenged this decision and the UN withdrew its recognition.

Lambda Legal Defense and Education Fund was founded in 1973 and has chapters in New York, Chicago, and Los Angeles. LLDEF is dedicated to protecting the rights of gays and lesbians through litigation and to antigay discrimination education.

Log Cabin Federation was founded in 1990 and grew quickly from the original eight chapters to thirty-two to become a league of gay and lesbian Republican clubs with a national conservative lobby.

Human Rights Campaign Fund, the largest gay and lesbian political organization, was founded in 1980 and lobbies in Washington for gay and lesbian rights, helps elect progay and lesbian legislators, and mobilizes grassroots support for the cause.

National Gay and Lesbian Task Force, another leading gay and lesbian rights advocacy group founded in 1973, battles antigay ballot initiatives, combats violence against gays and lesbians, lobbies for rights legislation, educates on the issues, and organizes on the grassroots level.

RESOURCES

Log Cabin Republicans
1101 14th St. NW
Washington, DC 20005
202-347-5306
fax: 202-347-5224

Human Rights Campaign Fund
(see page 106)

Gay and Lesbian Independent Democrats
c/o The Center
208 West 13th St.
New York, NY 10011
212-727-0008

Gay and Lesbian Victory Fund
1012 14th St. NW, Suite 1000
Washington, DC 20005
202-842-8679
fax: 202-289-3863

International Gay and Lesbian Association
c/o The Center
208 West 13th St.
New York, NY 10011
212-620-7310

32
Build Coalitions

An antigay ballot measure passed in Cincinnati with heavy
support from black ministers and their parishioners.
—*THE NEW YORK TIMES 12/13/94*

BACKGROUND

Prominent sociologists have always maintained that if there is
one truism in social psychology, it's that a person who's prejudiced toward one group is prejudiced toward another. Certain
groups in society have historically found themselves the subject
of hatred and scapegoating. In the United States African-
Americans, Jews, Native-Americans, gay men and lesbians,
women, and Hispanics are among such groups and all have organized to protect their rights and themselves from the attack of
bigots with power. Unification and organization is a fundamental strategy for a successful civil rights movement. Building
broad coalitions with other minority groups is another. Coalitions among oppressed groups help prevent the majority from
subjugating minorities with divide-and-conquer tactics. When
minority groups turn against each other, they are playing into
the hands of the oppressors and place the rights of all minorities
in danger. Organizations with a common enemy that fail to

build and maintain strong and enduring coalitions with each other leave gaps that can be penetrated, causing minority groups to fight each other instead of the more dangerous and powerful common enemy.

On December 13, 1993, *The New York Times* reported that religious right organizations, including Coloradans for Family Values, worked vigorously to get African-Americans to support an antigay and lesbian initiative that was on the ballot in Cincinnati in 1993. Fifty-six percent of African-Americans voted for the initiative. The measure passed, but it was declared unconstitutional in August 1994. Gays and lesbians should learn from the Cincinnati situation that they must build strong coalitions with other minority groups. Building coalitions can prevent misunderstandings and overcome differences that divide. For example, over the past few years there has increasingly been misguided debate among certain elements in the Jewish and African-American communities over who is more oppressed, which group has had the worst of it. The religious right is aware of this debate and how effectively this bickering has divided both communities, and is now distributing homophobic propaganda in African-American communities to promote a similar conflict between gays and lesbians and African-Americans. Debates over the degree of oppression between groups is counterproductive, ridiculous, and tends to glorify oppression. It is obvious that different minority groups are oppressed in different ways and to varying degrees, but they need to focus on what unites instead of what divides. Different minorities have issues that are unique to them, and it is important for others to understand them and support and participate in each other's struggle against the racist, anti-Semitic, sexist, and homophobic forces. It is for this reason that you become involved in gay and lesbian organizations and assist them with building coalitions and maintaining coalitions that already exist.

Things to Do

- Find a minority organization working for civil rights in your community and make contact with their representative.
- Organize a meeting where you will discuss shared experiences with discrimination, current issues, goals, and strategies.
- Develop an activist relationship with a member of the other group, maintaining frequent contact and constantly updating each other on the issues.
- Minority groups should educate each other about the stereotypes and common myths used to keep each group in its place and on the defensive.
- Gay and lesbian groups alone are not responsible for building alliances. All minority groups should reach out to the gay and lesbian community, especially now that it is under siege.
- Don't keep your alliances a secret. They send strong messages to politicians and community leaders of your mutual support and dedication to each other's cause.
- Coalition groups should participate in each other's demonstrations, boycotts, and petition drives and share information on politicians and businesses.
- Gay and lesbian organizations should strive to demonstrate the diversity within the community and ensure that the power within the organization is distributed and shared by gays and lesbians from all ethnic, social, and economic groups.
- Labor unions and large civil rights organizations like the Center for Democratic Renewal and Amnesty International should not be overlooked as important alliances.
- Develop your own individual coalitions: discuss gay and lesbian issues with your minority friends and listen to their opinions.
- Join minority organizations and read their newsletters.

RESOURCES

AFL-CIO
815 16th St. NW
Washington, DC 20006
202-637-5000

Amnesty International, USA
"Breaking the Silence" Newsletter
322 8th Ave.
New York, NY 10001
212-807-8400

Anti-Defamation League of B'nai B'rith
823 UN Plaza
New York, NY 10017
212-490-2525

Center for Democratic Renewal
P.O. Box 50469
Atlanta, GA 30302
404-221-0025

Latino Rights Project
666 Broadway, Rm. 625
New York, NY 10012
212-722-1645

National Association for the Advancement of Colored People (NAACP)
1025 Vermont Ave. NW
Washington, DC 20035
202-638-2269

National Organization for Women (NOW)
1000 16th St. NW Suite 700
Washington, DC 20036
202-331-0066

33
Register and Vote

BACKGROUND

The number of active voters in the United States is far lower than in any western democracy. There are two main reasons why this substantial group of eligible voters have disenfranchised themselves. Some are disinterested in the political process and take the right to vote for granted; others are cynical and apathetic about politics and politicians and believe that their vote won't make a difference. If you take the right to vote for granted, you need to learn the consequences of being really disenfranchised. Every time you fail to cast a ballot you are handing over your power to another person, allowing him or her to make decisions that will affect your life and well-being; you are weakening and they are becoming strong. Your only hope is that the active voter is a tolerant and just individual who will vote for tolerant politicians. The best way to avoid this precarious situation is to hold onto your power and political expression by participating fully in the political process and voting. Voting is not a difficult task, yet it is the most important action you can take to protect gay and lesbian rights.

Those of you who are cynical and apathetic about the political process and politicians should understand that not all politicians are same. Some have different values and promote different causes; some support gay and lesbian rights and others are homophobic and do not. Progressive candidates and civil liberties are the big losers when cynicism and voter apathy takes hold of the population. The reactionaries are always interested in politics and passionate enough to take their cause to the ballot box. They elect homophobes like themselves, and you are victimized not only by your own cynicism, but also by intolerant politicians with power. You can prevent this victimization by becoming as passionate about your cause as the "traditional values" people are about theirs. Gays, lesbians, and their supporters can keep antigay and lesbian politicians out of office by voting for individuals who support the movement.

Many people feel that if they vote in the national elections for president, senators, and congresspeople that they have done their duty. While these major elections are important, local elections are crucial when it comes to gay and lesbian rights. The religious right knows that local authorities like judges, council, and school board members enforce the values of a community and establish policies. For years the religious right has worked diligently on the local level to fill elected positions with homophobic politicians who have attacked the rights of gays and lesbians at the grassroots level. This attack on gay and lesbian rights can be prevented when you decide that you want to participate and elect officials who reflect the values of the entire community, not just a minority of reactionaries.

Things to Do

- Register to vote.
- Find out how to register. Each state has voter registration information lines and each district has a local board of elections. Call them.

- If you are an American citizen over eighteen and have never been convicted of a felony, then you should encounter no restrictions on your right to register and vote. Should you encounter any, file a protest at the board of elections and ask them to investigate.

- If you have to travel during election time, don't forget to obtain an absentee ballot before you leave on the trip.

- Become involved in voter drives at election time.

- Research the candidates and become an educated voter. Know exactly who you are voting for and what their views are on issues that effect gays, lesbians, and other minority communities. Call their campaign headquarters and ask specific questions on the issues that concern you. If they are indifferent or opposed to gay and lesbian rights, let them know that their position will cost them your vote and others. It is important for politicians to know that their position on gay and lesbian rights could affect the outcome of the election.

- Know everything there is to know about the initiatives on the ballot, including what the consequences are of these new ordinances and laws. Listen to what both sides of the issues are saying.

- Don't wait until election day to become informed. Work diligently in advance to ensure you have the necessary information.

- Remind friends and relatives to register and vote.

- Focusing on gay and lesbian rights, give them information on the ballot initiatives and the candidates running for office. Also, tell your family and friends how antigay and lesbian politicians hurt the gay and lesbian community.

- Remember, there is no such thing as an unimportant election. You are affected by all political offices no matter how large or small.

- Be sure to get to the polls on election day, avoiding using feeble excuses like bad weather to stay at home.

RESOURCES

Center for Voting and Democracy
6905 5th Ave. NW, #200
Washington, DC 20012
202-882-7378

The League of Women Voters
1730 M St. NW
Washington, DC 20036
202-429-1965

34
Call, Write, or Visit
Your Representatives

BACKGROUND

Gay and lesbian rights issues appear frequently before all branches of government on both the state and federal levels. Your senators and representatives in the House vote one way or another on these issues. As elected officials, their duty is to know the will of their constituents and to vote accordingly. Unless, however, you take the time to voice your support for gay and lesbian rights your representatives will hear only from the vocal antigay and lesbian forces and probably vote against gay causes. When President Clinton proposed lifting the ban on gays in the military, the religious right organized a letter-writing campaign and phone zap of the White House that was so effective it prompted the president to hesitate and reconsider his proposal. Had gays, lesbians, and their supporters shown the same intensity and made the same concerted effort the gays-in-the-military issue could have concluded favorably: the president would have lifted the ban unconditionally instead of settling for the "don'task, don't-tell" compromise. Other instances will occur in the future and provide gays and lesbians the opportunity to demonstrate that they too have an opinion and a vote.

Never doubt that politicians pay attention to their mail and phone calls. By communicating with them, you have the ability to influence their position on important issues. Your letter or phone call notifies your senators and representatives that they have constituents who support gay and lesbian rights and who pay attention to how they vote. Sending this powerful message takes very little effort. A great deal can be accomplished by simply writing a letter and picking up the phone. Many people are unsure about how to compose a letter to their representatives or perhaps they suffer from writer's block; for this reason, I enclose the following letter as a guide:

SAMPLE LETTER

(Your name and address)
(Date)
The Honorable ———
U.S. House of Representatives
Washington, DC 20515

Dear Congressperson ———,
I respectfully urge you to support the Employee Nondiscrimination Act (ENA), which was introduced in Congress this year. Discrimination based on sexual orientation is widespread in our society. While gays and lesbians need legal protection from all forms of discrimination, the ENA will protect their fundamental right to work and support themselves and their families.

Recently, three members of congress publicly acknowledged that they would not knowingly hire gay or lesbian staffers. Even these congressmen, who are entrusted with the important task of representing the people, discriminate based on sexual orientation. This disclosure in itself underscores the need for the enactment of the ENA.

While some jurisdictions around the country have enacted laws that protect gays and lesbians, these laws are under attack. Antigay and lesbian organizations have banded together and through the use of propaganda are convincing voters to repeal laws. In 1993 alone gay and lesbian rights legislation was repealed in three districts. The ENA will provide gay people with proper and decisive recourse to challenge employment discrimination.

Sincerely,

Things to Do

• You want to influence your representatives, not bore or irritate them. Your letter should have a personal style, convey your opinion in a polite tone, and be as brief as possible. Wordy letters are boring and tedious and may not leave a strong impression on your congressperson.

• Get to the point immediately by stating your purpose in the first sentence. Clarify and explain your concerns about the issue.

• Send copies of your letter to more than one politician.

• Show your letter to friends and relatives and encourage them to copy the letter or write their own. Be sure to supply them with the facts on the issues.

• When you call your representatives, know what you are

going to say before you call. Have the facts at hand and be prepared to express yourself in a firm but polite tone.

- Call the offices on a regular basis to express your support for gay and lesbian rights.

- Circulate the congressional phone numbers and encourage friends, family, and coworkers to call supporting gay and lesbian rights legislation.

- Learn the voting record of your congresspeople. *The Congressional Quarterly*, which can be found in most good libraries, lists the congressional roll call.

- In addition to writing letters and making phone calls, bombard legislatures with postcards and mailgrams immediately before a vote on legislation concerning gay and lesbian rights. Send postcards in the name of friends if you can't motivate them to do it, but get their permission first.

- Don't ignore your state senators and representatives. You can find out who they are by calling the legislative offices in your state capitol.

RESOURCES

President Bill Clinton
The White House
1600 Pennsylvania Avenue
Washington, DC 20003
202-456-1111
fax: 202-456-2461

House of Representatives
Washington, DC 20515
202-225-3644

The Senate
Washington, DC 20515
202-224-3207

35
Evaluate Institutional Homophobia in Businesses and Organizations

BACKGROUND

Institutional homophobia exists in some organizations and businesses and it directly affects the status of gays and lesbians in society. Homophobic policies and attitudes deprive gays and lesbians of the basic rights that most heterosexuals take for granted. You can evaluate an organization or business and determine whether or not its policies and attitude are homophobic. Conduct this evaluation before you join an organization, invest in a business, or buy its products. It is self-defeating for gay and lesbian rights supporters to give their financial resources to homophobic institutions. Unfortunately, you cannot prevent your tax dollars from going to homophobic governmental organizations like the Pentagon, but you do have control over the allocation of your assets in the private sector. Simply calling or writing to a business or organization and inquiring about their attitudes is useless. They will invariably deny that they are homophobic. You have to determine their position on your own.

Things to Do

- *Advertising*. The type of advertising campaign that a company uses to sell its products can give you clues as to the company's attitude. Advertising campaigns project the image of the company. By analyzing the content of an ad, reading the copy, listening to the dialogue for slogans or attitude-indicating phrases, observing the type of actors or models they use and who their spokesperson is, you can determine the company's image and to whom their advertising is directed. Macho, sexist, or racist images could be an indication that the company also has a negative attitude toward gays and lesbians.

- *Nondiscrimination policies and domestic partnership benefits*. Approximately 38 percent of large corporations have included sexual orientation in their written nondiscrimination policies. Some progressive companies extend medical benefits to domestic partners of employees. To determine whether a company includes sexual orientation or offers domestic partnership benefits, call their public relations department at the corporate headquarters. If they confirm inclusion of sexual orientation, ask them to send you a copy of their nondiscrimination policy.

- *Board of directors*. Find out who sits on their board and, if possible, their political, social, and cultural affiliations. You can get this information from the corporation's annual report. Annual reports can be obtained either in libraries or through stockbrokers. You can get valuable information about organizations in their annual reports.

- *Political campaign donations*. Companies often donate funds to politicians they wish to see elected. Choose two or three of the most homophobic politicians and research their campaign records. For example, Senator Jesse Helms (R-NC), and Representative Robert Dornan (R-CA) are two archenemies of the gay and lesbian rights movement. Helms has made numerous homophobic statements over the excruciatingly long years he's been in office. In May 1993, he explained that the reason he opposed Clinton's nomination of Roberta Achtenberg for assistant secretary for the Department of Housing and Urban Development was "because she is a damn lesbian. I'm not going to put a lesbian in a position like that." He opposes all gay and lesbian rights legislation, claiming that "their [homosexuals] aim is to have the American people accept the proposition that their perverted lifestyle is worthy of protection. . . ." Dornan is just as bigoted as Helms. One of his many offenses took place in April 1994 when he made a personal attack on fellow representative Steve Gunderson (R-WI) during a house debate. Referring to Gunderson's sexual orientation, Dornan said "He's out. He's in. He's out. He's in. Now I guess you're out because you went and spoke at a huge homosexual dinner." Although personal attacks on fellow members during congressional debates are considered taboo, Dornan obviously feels that gay and lesbian representatives are fair game. It was Dornan who made the now infamous "lesbian spear-chuckers" comment while discussing those opposed to his reelection in 1993. When you research the campaign records of these two politicians, you will discover which corporations contribute to their election campaigns. Then ask yourself, "Do I want to do business with companies that help put these men in office?" You can find the campaign records of politicians in research libraries.

- *Contributions and sponsorship.* Businesses and organizations often sponsor or cosponsor events and donate to other organizations. Find out what type of events the corporations sponsor and to whom they donate. Do they contribute to organizations fighting for human rights or invest in a socially conscious way? Also, to what extent does the business or organization reach out to or cave into the religious right?

- Contact Progressive Asset Management and Ed Mickens for further and updated information about American companies with progressive or regressive policies toward gays and lesbians.

• Add your name to the Progressive Asset Management mailing list and receive the "Lavender Curtain" newsletter.

RESOURCES

Howard Tharsing (information about investing)
Progressive Asset Management
1814 Franklin St.
Oakland, CA 94612
510-834-3722

Ed Mickens
WorkLine
P.O. Box 2079
New York, NY 10128

36

Challenge Corporations with Regressive Policies Toward Gays and Lesbians

Boycotts are an interesting political tool and something that should be ideally suited to lesbians and gay men, considering our potential economic clout.

—ED MICKENS

(*Note:* The information on the companies discussed in sections 36 and 37 came from Howard Tharsing at Progressive Asset Management, GLAAD, and my own records.)

BACKGROUND

Gay and lesbian rights supporters have the power to challenge corporations that have homophobic attitudes and policies. They can express their dissatisfaction by writing to or calling the company or by simply using their buying power. Selling products is the reason why businesses exist, whether these products are items or media programs. Unless enough people buy its product a company will have difficulty surviving. Consumers have the luxury of having choices and can be selective when they shop in supermarkets or department stores, travel, watch TV, or dine out. You should use your economic leverage in the marketplace to fight homophobia in businesses and organizations.

Boycotts or threats of boycotts are an effective way to get corporations to take notice. Antigay and lesbian rights forces have been doing it for years and in many instances have successfully used the threat of boycott to pressure advertisers into with-drawing support from gay and lesbian programming on TV. This is why TV networks either avoid programs with gay and lesbian themes or notify their advertisers before airing these programs. Advertisers can then choose whether or not to take a chance and promote their products during the program. Some advertis-ers are willing to take chances, but for many the fear of a boycott is too great. For example, a recent gay and lesbian special on Comedy Central prompted thirteen advertisers who usually ad-vertise during the time slot to withdraw their advertising. If the homophobes successfully use boycotting as a weapon, so can les-bians and gays. You have the financial clout to make corpora-tions feel the repercussions of excluding gays and lesbians. It seems that some corporations do not realize that millions of peo-ple support gay and lesbian rights and that many of these buy their products. It's time to let them know.

Below is a list of companies cited by gay rights activists for discrimination or for having antigay attitudes. These companies should not necessarily be boycotted, but you should be aware of the offense and monitor them in case of future violations.

American Airlines
P.O. Box 619616
Dallas/Ft. Worth Airport,
TX 75261
800-433-7300
fax: 817-967-3816

Good Housekeeping
959 8th Ave.
New York, NY 10019
212-649-2000
fax: 212-977-9824

Kmart
3100 W. Big Beaver Rd.
Troy, MI 48084
810-643-1000
fax: 810-643-5249

Kraft General Foods, Inc.
Three Lakes Drive
Northfield, IL 60093-2753
708-998-2000
fax: 708-646-6836

The New York Daily News
220 East 42nd St.
New York, NY 10017
212-210-2100
fax: 212-949-3062

Shell Oil Co.
P.O. Box 2463
Houston, TX 77252
713-241-6161
fax: 713-241-3190

American Airlines has run into trouble with the gay and lesbian community. Activists cite two incidents that they consider offensive to gays. The first involved a gay man with AIDS who was forced by the flight crew to disembark in Chicago. The passenger sued and the case was settled out of court. The second incident occurred in April 1994 in Dallas. After a group of gay and lesbian passengers disembarked, a member of the crew requested a complete change of pillows and blankets "due to gay activists on board." This request was recorded by the tower and American was forced to apologize. American Airlines is now reaching out to the gay and lesbian community in an attempt to improve relations, but it will take time before it can be determined whether or not the company has actually changed its attitude.

Good Housekeeping was targeted by GLAAD/NY for excluding gays and lesbians from its 1993 promotional campaign geared toward nontraditional families. Although *Good Housekeeping* did not discriminate, its failure to recognize gay and lesbian households continues the historical exclusion of gays from society.

Kmart refused to stock Magic Johnson's AIDS prevention book *What You Can Do to Avoid AIDS.*

Kraft pulled advertising from the episode of *Roseanne* with the lesbian kiss.

The New York Daily News continues to stand by its columnist Mike McAlary, who in April 1994 incorrectly reported that a rape victim who happens to be a lesbian "has an active imagination" and fabricated the rape story to get publicity for a gay and lesbian rights rally. Even when the police revealed that lab reports indicated that the woman was indeed raped, McAlary continued to stand by his story and refused to apologize for his false allegation. The rape victim has filed a libel suit against McAlary and the newspaper.

Shell Oil fired an employee for being gay and was sued. The employee won the suit and was awarded three million dollars.

The following companies are repeat offenders. They have shown a complete indifference to the rights of gays and lesbians and are unresponsive to the protests of activists and others offended by their homophobia. You should *boycott* these four companies:

Boy Scouts of America
P.O. Box 152079
1325 W. Walnut Hill Lane
Irving, TX 75015-2079
214-580-2000
fax: 214-580-2502

Cracker Barrel Old
Country Store, Inc.
P.O. Box 787
Lebanon, TN 37088-0787
615-444-5533
fax: 615-443-6780

The Florida Citrus Commission
P.O. Box 148
Lakeland, FL 33802-0148
813-682-0171
fax: 813-499-2374

The New York Post
210 South Street
New York, NY 10002
212-815-8000

Florida Citrus is bad news all around. It is a conservative company that supports the "family values" movement and sponsors the religious right. Florida Citrus has demonstrated that it has not changed since it appointed Anita Bryant its spokesperson back in the 1970s. Bryant became notorious back in the late '70s when she led an antigay and lesbian rights campaign in Dade County, Florida. In 1994, Florida Citrus again demonstrated its love for homophobes when it named Rush Limbaugh, that vile hatemonger, as its spokesperson. After appointing Limbaugh the company's sales dropped and it did not reappoint him. This, however, does not mean that Florida Citrus has changed.

The New York Post is a homophobic rag. The *Post* regularly publishes editorials, offensive cartoons and articles that attack gays and lesbians and promote homophobic stereotypes. Since I first began monitoring *The Post* in 1990 I have never seen an editorial that supports gay and lesbian rights. The newspaper opposed lifting the ban on gays and lesbians in the military. Among its columnists is Ray Kerrison who is relentless in his attacks on the gay community. In June 1994, Kerrison wrote a column attacking Mayor Giuliani for his participating in the gay pride march.

Don't buy *The Post*, don't advertise in *The Post* and don't support its advertisers.

Cracker Barrel Old Country Stores, Inc: Refer to chapter 25 for a detailed account of the situation at this company.

The Boy Scouts of America has a written policy that bars membership to gays and lesbians. The Boy Scouts have been challenged in court. In 1980 a gay man sued when his sexual orientation prevented him from becoming a scoutmaster. He lost the case in 1994 when the Second District Court of Appeals in California ruled in favor of the Boy Scouts. The court asserted that "the imposition of a leader who is an improper role model is a severe intrusion upon First Amendment activities of an expressive association." The Boy Scouts vehemently defend this policy and make it clear that they fight all opposition to their homophobic discrimination.

Things to Do

• Write to these companies and express your concern about their discrimination against gays and lesbians and their regressive policies.

- Inform the four boycott targets that you are boycotting them.
- Encourage friends, family members, and acquaintances to do the same.
- Support official boycotts called by gay and lesbian organizations.

37

Support Corporations with Progressive Attitudes Toward Gays and Lesbians

AT&T is trying to make a name for itself with gay consumers.

—ADVERTISING AGE

BACKGROUND

The unity and activism of gays and lesbians has resulted in the formation of a group that the business community has to deal with. Some corporations are reluctant to reach out to gays and lesbians, fearing the wrath of homophobic organizations and individuals. Others, however, being shrewd and brave, have done the right thing and acknowledged the potential of the gay and lesbian market. Not only do many corporations demonstrate progressive marketing attitudes but they also implement inclusive policies for their gay and lesbian employees. They add the phrase "sexual orientation" to nondiscrimination policies and extend medical benefits to domestic partners. In addition, they tolerate and welcome gay and lesbian employee organizations and promote diversity training within their company to teach tolerance and respect for all minorities.

Homophobic organizations constantly intimidate progressive corporations to change their gay- and lesbian-inclusive policies. They organize letter-writing campaigns, phone zaps, and boycotts, hoping that strong negative responses will pressure these corporations into backsliding. For example, Apple Computer wanted to build an office complex in Williamson County, Texas, but the county's commissioners, citing Apple's policy of granting health benefits to domestic partners, refused to give the company a property tax abatement. They claimed Apple's policy promotes homosexuality. Apple resisted the coercion, threatened to go elsewhere, and won the tax abatement. Gay and lesbian rights supporters must provide the positive, encouraging response that progressive corporations like Apple Computer deserve.

Following is an example of the ideal nondiscrimination policy:

The ———— Company reaffirms its commitment to the principle of equal employment opportunity in its policies and practices. It is this company's policy to hire, train, and promote into all job levels employees and applicants for employment without regard to race, color, religion, gender, sexual orientation, national origin, and disability. Decisions are based on an individual's qualifications, competence, and merit.

Below is a list of some of the corporations you should support by buying their products and writing letters:

Apple Computer Inc.
1 Infinite Loop
Cupertino, CA 95016
408-996-1010

Apple offers full benefits for same-sex partners, has a nondiscrimination policy that includes sexual orientation, advertises in gay publications, and recognizes its gay and lesbian employees group.

AT&T Co.
32 Avenue of the Americas
New York, NY 10013
212-387-5400
fax: 212-841-4649

AT&T includes sexual orientation in its nondiscrimination policy, contributed funds to the Gay Games, and actively reaches out to the gay and lesbian market.

Ben & Jerry's Homemade, Inc.
P.O. Box 240
Waterbury, VT 05676
802-244-6957
fax: 802-244-1175

Ben & Jerry's offers full benefits to partners of gay and lesbian employees.

Colgate Palmolive Co.
300 Park Ave.
New York, NY 10022-7499
212-310-2000
fax: 212-310-3405

Colgate Palmolive includes sexual orientation in its nondiscrimination policy, and is reviewing benefits for domestic partners.

MCA/Universal
100 Universal City Plaza
Universal City, CA 91608
818-777-1000
fax: 818-777-8227

MCA/Universal includes sexual orientation in its nondiscrimination policy and offers full benefits to same-sex partners.

>Microsoft Corp.
>One Microsoft Way
>Redmond, WA 98052-6399
>206-882-8080
>fax: 206-936-7329

Microsoft includes sexual orientation in its nondiscrimination policy and offers full benefits to same-sex partners.

>Time Warner, Inc.
>75 Rockefeller Plaza
>New York, NY 10019
>212-484-8000
>fax: 212-956-2847

Warner Bros. offers full benefits to same-sex partners, but Time does not.

>Viacom Inc.
>1515 Broadway
>New York, NY 10036
>212-258-6000
>fax: 212-258-6354

Viacom offers full benefits to same-sex partners.

RESOURCES

Mickens, Ed. *The 100 Best Companies for Gay Men and Lesbians.* New York: Pocket Books, 1994.

Woods, James D. *The Corporate Closet.* New York: The Free Press, 1993.

38
Know Your Enemy: The Religious Right

If you are truly right within your heart and with Christianity, you know in advance that you do not know enough about other people's lives to judge them.
—Dr. Joycelyn Elders

Judge not that ye not be judged.
—Matthew, VII, 1, 2

BACKGROUND

The gay and lesbian rights movement has achieved enormous success since the Stonewall Rebellion. This success, however, has prompted the homophobic forces to band together in an attempt to obstruct the movement's progress and force gays and lesbians back into the closet. The history of all civil rights movements reveals that when minority groups start attaining their rights a backlash ensues. For example, a right-wing backlash almost destroyed the feminist movement during the struggle over the Equal Rights Amendment, and as a result the word *feminist* became taboo in the 1980s, forcing many women at the time to distance themselves from the movement by making silly statements like "I'm not a feminist, but . . ." Fortunately, the feminist movement survived and, in the 1990s, has regained support and strength. The backlash against the gay and lesbian rights movement is orchestrated primarily by the fearmongers and hatemongers of the religious right.

The religious right is a blanket term that encompasses a variety of powerful organizations. I believe that the goal of these organizations is to gain political power and destroy America's commitment to the separation of church and state. The founders of this country endorsed the separation of church and state, realizing that this separation is necessary for maintaining religious and secular freedom. The religious right knows that by pandering to Middle America's ignorance and fear of gays and lesbians the membership in its organizations increases and they become richer. Thus, they generate and circulate in communities around the country hateful propaganda such as *The Gay Agenda*, a vile antigay and lesbian video that is filled with lies and distortions intended to dehumanize gay people and frighten heterosexuals. The religious right scapegoats gays and lesbians, blaming them for everything from the deterioration of so-called traditional family values to the Los Angeles earthquake of 1994.

Needless to say, the deceitful tactics of the religious right have proven to be successful. The situation is critical. In the past few years the religious right convinced voters to pass antigay and lesbian ballot measures in Oregon, Colorado, New Hampshire, Maine, and Ohio, and this year it introduced ballot initiatives in other states that would legalize discrimination on the basis of sexual orientation. The religious right threatens not only the rights of gays and lesbians but the freedom of all Americans. Thus it is vital for everyone who values justice to challenge this movement, to prevent themselves and others from being misled by propaganda, and to expose and take action against its un-American agenda.

Beware of the organizations listed below. They are the most powerful groups associated with the religious right:

American Family Association
Donald Wildmon
P.O. Box 2440
Tupelo, MS 38803
601-844-5036

The Christian Coalition
Pat Robertson
P.O. Box 1990
Chesapeake, VA 23327
804-424-2630

Concerned Women for America
Beverly LaHaye
901 D St. SW, # 800
Washington, DC 20024
202-488-7000

Family Research Council
Gary Bauer
700 13th St. NW #500
Washington, DC 20005
202-393-2100

Focus on the Family
James Dobson
P.O. Box 35500
Colorado Springs, CO 80935
719-531-3400

Tradition Values Coalition
Lou Sheldon
P. O. Box 940
Anaheim, CA 92815
714-520-0300

In addition to NGLTF, GLAAD, the American Civil Liberties Union, and the Lambda Legal Defense and Education Fund, the following organizations work against the religious right and deserve your support:

Americans United for Separation of Church and State
1816 Jefferson Pl. NW
Washington, DC 20036
202-466-3234

Center for Democratic Renewal
P.O. Box 50469
Atlanta, GA 30302
404-221-0025
(Keeps track of hate groups and publishes a bimonthly newsletter, "*The Monitor.*")

Institute for First Amendment Studies
P.O. Box 589
Great Barrington, MA 01230
413-528-3800

People for the American Way
2000 M St. NW, # 400
Washington, DC 20036
202-467-4999

Things to Do

• *Never* underestimate the power of the Religious Right; its organizations are well organized and funded, and their combined membership is in the millions. Recently the media has legitimized their agenda by giving them air time and allowing their spokespeople to participate in political debates.

• Be on the alert for hateful propaganda and lies and inform others of its existence.

• Educate your friends, acquaintances, coworkers, and family members concerning the real agenda of the religious right and its underhanded tactics.

• If you know someone who is a member or supporter of the religious right, inform him or her of its true agenda, that it is based on un-American doctrine that could deprive citizens of freedom, justice, and civil rights. Encourage them to withdraw their membership and support.

• Call and write to the religious right organizations listed above. Let them know that you are onto them, that you consider their convictions to be abhorrent and distorted.

• Organize or participate in demonstrations at their headquarters.

• Contact the National Gay and Lesbian Task Force at 202-332-6483 and ask them to send you a copy of their *Fight the Right* action kit.

• If antigay and lesbian initiatives are on the ballot in your state, vote against them and tell others to do the same.

• Join organizations listed above that fight the religious right and become a volunteer in their offices.

RESOURCES

Helminiak, Daniel A. *What the Bible Really Says About Homosexuality.* San Francisco: Alamo Square Press, 1994.

Herick, Gregory M., ed. *Hate Crimes: Confronting Violence Against Lesbians and Gays.* London: Sage, 1992.

Plant, Richard. *The Pink Triangle: The Nazi War Against Homosexuals.* New York: Holt, 1989.

39
Learn How Cultural Homophobia Is Harmful

I was told that I would get my butt kicked or bashed if I took my date to my school prom.
—PAUL RIVERA, GAY TEENAGER

BACKGROUND

Cultural homophobia is also known as heterosexism and it pertains to the cultural mores and standards that arise from the belief that heterosexuality is superior and thus preferable to homosexuality. Heterosexism perpetuates the myth that everyone is heterosexual, and it explains the existence of gays and lesbians by maintaining that they are antisocial deviants who need rehabilitation. The assumption that everyone is heterosexual results in total heterosexual domination over romantic representations and social codes of behavior, preserves heterosexual privilege, and excludes anyone who is not heterosexual from honestly representing themselves and participating in the mainstream social, political, historical, and cultural environment, therefore rendering them invisible. Evidence of cultural homophobia exists everywhere. It manifests every day on television where just about every romantic situation involves heterosexuals. The two or three exceptions that depict gay or lesbian ro-

166

mance do so under restrictions, such as no kissing allowed, that are not applied to heterosexuals. Cultural homophobia is evident in advertising, publishing, movies, and all media that portray human interaction and social relationship. These portraits invariably assume that everyone is attracted to, married to, or will eventually marry a member of the opposite sex. Where does all this leave the 10 percent of the population who don't fit the heterosexual mold? Excluded and forced into a subculture.

As with the other types of homophobia, gay and lesbian rights supporters have had some success combating cultural homophobia. But there is still a long way to go before gays and lesbians receive the representation that their population size deserves.

More Reasons Why Cultural Homophobia Is Harmful

• It forces people into rigid gender role playing. The abundance of heterosexual images in society reinforces male and female role playing. These images usually depict a dominant male and a submissive female. Role playing can be a burden on both genders.

• It compels some gays and lesbians to betray their true nature and behave like heterosexuals.

• It is a waste of energy. The amount of energy spent on suppressing and concealing gay and lesbian relationships could be put to better use.

• It promotes negative stereotypes and causes ignorance of diversity.

• It deprives gays and lesbians of the satisfaction of seeing depictions of relationships they can relate to in the mainstream.

Examples of Cultural Homophobia

• Destroying or censoring art with gay or lesbian themes. For example, the early Christian church officials had access to the manuscripts of Sappho's poems and their hostility toward lesbianism prompted them to destroy most of her poetry. Only two poems survived intact; the rest are fragments discovered by archaeologists. Also, E. M. Forster wrote his homosexual novel *Maurice* in 1914, but, fearing the consequences, he refused to have it published during his lifetime. It remained unpublished until 1971.

• Concealing the homosexuality of famous people. Since 10 percent of the population is gay and lesbian, it follows that 10 percent of accomplished and famous individuals are also gay and lesbian. But you would never know this if you depended on biographers. While biographers diligently research and reveal the private lives of heterosexual subjects they generally tend to ignore the sexual orientation of closeted gay and lesbian subjects even when they know the truth. Instead they continue to perpetuate the big lie, the marriages of convenience and the phony heterosexual affairs that many famous gays and lesbians hid, and still continue to hide, behind.

• Excluding out gays and lesbians from the mainstream and forcing them to live in gay ghettos. Openly gay and lesbian people are subjected to so much hostility from the mainstream that in order to feel safe, many choose to live in cities and districts with large gay populations.

Things to Do

• Reject images that assume everyone is heterosexual.

• Contact institutions like TV networks that promote cultural homophobia and ask them to provide nonstereotypical depictions of gays and lesbians.

• Refuse to remain invisible. Interact openly in public with your companion and demonstrate through example the diversity of humanity.

• Heterosexuals should try to imagine what it would be like if the situation was reversed and 99.9 percent of cultural images represented gay and lesbian interaction.

40
Know the Facts: Distinguish Between Myth and Reality

BACKGROUND

There are obvious reasons why heterosexual society creates and maintains myths about gays and lesbians and their experience. First, many heterosexuals are profoundly ignorant of the actual experience of gays and lesbians, and when people are ignorant they tend to spend precious time filling the void with useless and destructive information. It is easier for them to believe the old rubbish handed down by parents or grandparents than to invest time in discovering the truth. Second, homophobia, like all forms of oppression, is the weapon used by the dominant heterosexual group to institute and maintain power over the gay and lesbian minority. Heterosexuals sustain oppressive behavior and retain a false belief system in order to gain approval from their peers and avoid ridicule, to feel superior, and to categorize sexuality in an attempt to simplify this complex subject.

Gay and lesbian rights supporters must be on the alert for the myths that heterosexuals use to exclude sexual minorities from the mainstream. Homophobic people have carefully nurtured and developed false beliefs for centuries and they will not give them up easily; therefore, gays and lesbians must use every opportunity to deconstruct these myths. The only viable way to achieve this goal is to learn the facts surrounding the myth, and armed with the facts, use every chance to challenge the beliefs. Every time gays and lesbians destroy a myth about their sexuality they are moving a step closer to ending homophobia.

EXAMPLES OF MYTHS AND FACTS

Myth: Gays and lesbians already have civil rights. What they want is special rights.

Fact: Gays and lesbians want the same rights as heterosexuals, protection under the law from discrimination.

Myth: Homosexuality is unnatural and a depravity.

Fact: Homosexuality is a unique part of human nature and even exists in some animal species.

Myth: Lesbians are man haters.

Fact: Most lesbians don't hate men. Lesbianism is about women loving women.

Myth: Gay men hate women.

Fact: Some men, gay and straight, hate women. Everyone, regardless of gender or sexual orientation is capable of hating others.

Myth: Bisexuals are confused about their sexuality.

Fact: Many people, whether they know it or not, are bisexual to some degree. There is nothing confusing about being sexually attracted to both genders.

Myth: Gay and lesbian relationships don't last.

Fact: Many gay and lesbian couples maintain a lifelong committed relationship or relationships that last for many years. Heterosexuals form relationships that also vary in length.

Myth: Gays and lesbians can't reproduce so in order to increase their ranks they recruit children.

Fact: No one can be forced to be gay or lesbian. Homosexuality is innate and same-gender sexual attraction comes from within.

Myth: Gay men molest children.

Fact: Most child molestation cases involve heterosexual men preying on female children. Studies show that it is the children's fathers, stepfathers, and mother's boyfriends who molest children the most.

Myth: Lesbians and gays can be cured by changing their behavior and through therapy.

Fact: While a small number of gays and lesbians try to change their sexual orientation by changing their behavior, their fundamental homosexual desire always remains. They accomplish nothing constructive and only make themselves and the heterosexuals they become involved with miserable.

Things to Do

- Make a list of beliefs that you think are myths.
- Research information and statistics and provide examples that contradict and challenge each myth.
- Discuss the myth and its deconstruction with other gays and lesbians. Perhaps they know other myths that can also be deconstructed.
- Stop believing the myth. All your efforts will be fruitless if you continue to believe and perpetuate myths that promote homophobia.
- Challenge people who perpetuate myths about gays and lesbians. Most people who believe these myths don't realize that what they believe is untrue and will accept the truth when it is backed up by rational debate and facts. So spread the word. Many people are in need of education.

41
Fight Censorship of the Gay and Lesbian Experience

BACKGROUND

The shortage of positive representations of the gay and lesbian experience in mainstream society does not mean that people have neglected to depict these experiences. Many artists, writers, journalists, songwriters, and educators have portrayed gay and lesbian life, but in the past and to some degree in the present, censorship prevented mainstream society from having access to their work. The purpose of censorship is to control the thoughts and behavior of people. When the elements in power feel that certain ideas or representations threaten their power, they turn to censorship as a means of controlling and eliminating the threat. Some of the groups and individuals who have the power to censor or influence censors include local school boards, teachers, citizens' groups, media, motion picture and advertising executives, government agencies like the FCC, and organizations such as Focus on the Family.

In order to maintain the total domination of heterosexuality, material with gay and lesbian themes is often labeled "indecent or pornographic." Whether or not there is any sexual content is irrelevant. The mere mention of homosexuality or lesbianism is all that is necessary for a work to be censored or edited. For example, the producers of the 1951 movie version of Tennessee Williams's play, *A Streetcar Named Desire*, eliminated references to the homosexuality of Blanche du Bois's husband. Instead of centering the conflict on the character's homosexuality, as the playwright intended, the movie attributed the conflict to a nervous condition. But some may think that was 1951 and things are different now. While it's true that the situation has improved, gay- and lesbian-themed material still faces censorship in some quarters. In 1993, Canadian Customs confiscated copies of David Leavitt's book, *A Place I've Never Been*, and the lesbian-themed comic book *Hothead Paisan*. In 1990, the FCC issued a twenty-four-hour-a-day ban on all indecent material, including readings of Allen Ginsberg's acclaimed poem, *Howl*, which contains many references to homosexuality. Also, some newspapers dropped the comic strip *Doonesbury*, when Trudeau introduced a gay character and began dealing with gay issues.

Without freedom of speech and expression, the visibility of gays and lesbians will be jeopardized, stereotypes will thrive, mainstream society will remain ignorant about homosexuality and sexuality, and homophobia will continue to flourish.

Examples of Cultural Homophobic Censorship

• Failing to mention homosexuality and lesbianism in textbooks.

• Airing gay- or lesbian-themed programs late at night when most people are asleep.

• Altering pronouns in poetry, journals, and letters to eliminate traces of same-gender desire and romance. Emily Dickinson's letters were bowdlerized in this manner by her niece Martha Dickinson Bianchi, as were Michelangelo's love sonnets by his great-nephew.

- Actors refusing to play roles that involve same-gender relationships.
- Allowing gay and lesbian depictions only if they are stereotypical.
- Denying funding to organizations like the National Endowment for the Arts that include gay and lesbian artists in its grants.
- Refusing to stock gay and lesbian magazines, books, and newspapers.
- Refusing to print or distribute gay and lesbian books and magazines.
- Refusing to show gay- and lesbian-themed works of art.

Things to Do

- Buy and read the books and magazines that have been challenged by censors.
- Watch movies and TV programs that are controversial because of their gay and lesbian content.
- Although gay and lesbian marriages are not legally recognized, many couples still have commitment ceremonies. If you are planning a ceremony, send an announcement to the newspaper. Although the newspaper won't print it, they still should know that these events take place.
- Write to mainstream men's and women's magazines informing them that gays and lesbians exist (the editors of these magazines don't seem to know this), that they have similar concerns and interests as heterosexuals, and perhaps should be included in articles and editorials.
- Create a work of art that depicts the censorship of gay and lesbian experience.
- Contact your friends and acquaintances and begin a grassroots group to track and fight censorship. Plan a monthly meeting to discuss the latest issues and strategies. Start a newsletter.
- Call the evening talk shows on TV (CNBC, CNN, C-SPAN etc.) and discuss gay and lesbian invisibility and censor-

ship. Put the hosts on the spot by asking them why they rarely mention gays and lesbians or rights issues.

- Write or call the TV networks and ask them to stop censoring and also to show gay- and lesbian-themed movies. The major ones are listed below.
- Write to the FCC and demand that it lift the ban on so-called indecent programs.
- Give your support to the NEA. Tell them to continue funding art that depicts the gay and lesbian experience.

RESOURCES

ABC TV
30 West 66th St.
New York, NY 10023
212-456-1000

NBC TV
30 Rockefeller Plaza
New York, NY 10020
212-644-2333

Fox TV
205 East 67th St.
New York, NY 10021
212-452-3600

CBS, Inc.
51 West 52nd St.
New York, NY 10019
212-975-4321

Federal Communications Commission, Enforcement Division
Mass Media Bureau
1919 M St. NW
Washington, DC 20036

42
Free Yourself from Gender Stereotypes

Each of us is born with a full circle of human qualities, and
also with a unique version of them.

—GLORIA STEINEM

BACKGROUND

From the moment children are born they are conditioned according to the gender roles that society expects them to play. This conditioning becomes apparent as the child gets older, reflected in their behavior, appearance, and attitudes. Boys behave aggressively and physically, dress in unrestrictive clothing, and display an aura of confidence, while girls tend to be acquiescent, reticent, and lacking in self-confidence. Teachers and peers reinforce gender role playing, and should a child rebel and demonstrate behavior that is contrary to their conditioning as a male or female, they are punished, shunned, and derided with terms like *sissy* or *tomboy*. Nonconformity to gender stereotypes threatens the established patriarchal order of male dominance and female dependency, and society deals harshly with defiance. Nonconformists become victims of gay and lesbian baiting. This is particularly evident during the sensitive teenage years when boys with passive and reticent tendencies are labeled *fags* by their peers and girls who are aggressive, interested in sports, and good at math are called *dykes*.

The false assumption that individuals are gay and lesbian when they refuse to conform to gender role playing promotes homophobic stereotypes and deflects attention from the true reason for their resistance. Many people, heterosexuals and homosexuals, are individualists who strive to fulfill their total human potential. Their attempts often require them to reject the limited gender roles defined by society. Others, including some gays and lesbians, are comfortable with and accept gender role playing, and live within its guidelines.

The women's liberation movement and the gay and lesbian rights movement have created change that benefits everyone, straight men included, dedicated to individual freedom and expression. Not all men want to shoulder the burden of supporting the family. Some want to have the option of being the primary nurturers, tending the home and taking care of the children. The feminists' attack on gender role playing and gender division of labor has given men this opportunity, and many are taking advantage of it and enjoying its rewards. Also, the benefits of a nonhomophobic society include liberating men, straight and gay, so that they can interact freely with and demonstrate affection for other men without being gay baited.

Things to Do

• Parents and teachers should not restrict children's options by forcing them into gender role playing and depriving them of exploring their full human potential.

• Teach children not to taunt and shun peers who don't conform to gender roles.

• Give encouragement and support to young people struggling with gender role playing.

• Be true to yourself. Resist career limitations imposed by

gender roles. For example, the fear of being labeled a lesbian often deters heterosexual and lesbian women from pursuing careers in sports even when that's where their interest lies. Also, in order to avoid similar gay baiting heterosexual men may reject careers as fashion designers or hairdressers. By rejecting the gender division of labor, you will help change things and defuse the potency of gay and lesbian baiting, decrease homophobia, and free yourself from gender bondage.

• Dress in a manner that is comfortable for you. While it is necessary to conform to a dress code while on the job, in your private life you have the freedom to dress as you desire. Take advantage of this freedom regardless of people's disapproval. (Let's face it, men's clothing is more comfortable, less expensive, less complicated, less restricting, and presents an air of authority.)

• Examine hypermasculine and hyperfeminine behavior. It is transparent and indicates that the person is compensating for feeling inadequate regarding their gender role.

• Read in-depth studies on the issue of gender role playing and its connection to cultural homophobia.

43
Free Yourself from
Gay and Lesbian Stereotypes

*Stereotype: A fixed or conventional notion or
conception . . . held by a number of people, and allowing for
no individuality . . .*
—WEBSTER'S NEW WORLD DICTIONARY

BACKGROUND

All social, ethnic, and national groups cope with stereotypes that
others create in an effort to understand or demean different
groups. Although some stereotypes emerge from a fragment of
truth, this truth is embellished and develops into a distortion. For
example, it is true that some gay men are effeminate and some
lesbians are masculine, but the distortion occurs when these traits
are applied to the entire group. Other stereotypes have no basis
in truth and develop out of a need to justify racism, sexism, anti-
Semitism, and homophobia. Stereotypes, whether or not they
originate from a truth, become a weapon of oppression when the
dominant group uses them to keep minorities in their place.
They are an effective weapon insofar as some members of an oppressed group have a tendency to accept stereotypes* and incor-

*This discussion of gay and lesbian stereotypes in no way includes transgenderism or
transsexualism, nor does it imply that people of this nature conform to stereotypes. On
the contrary, transgender and transsexual people are true individualists who bravely reject gender stereotypes and express their true nature.

porate the assigned traits into their lives, thereby limiting their individuality and perpetuating the stereotype.

Some people still have stereotypical ideas of what homosexuals are supposed to look like. When Melissa Etheridge came out, a coworker of mine said, "She's gay? She doesn't look gay." When I asked her how she thought Melissa should look she was embarrassed and became aware of her misconception. Apparently she believed that all lesbians have short hair and never wear makeup.

As a sexual minority, gay men and lesbians have more than their share of stereotypes to contend with. Their past, and to some degree current, invisibility allows heterosexuals to define who gays and lesbians are in negative terms. They are defined, among other things, as sexual predators, misogynists and man haters, and antisocial deviants. Homophobes then use these stereotypes to excuse discrimination against gays and lesbians. For example, one justification for banning gays and lesbians from the military is that straight servicemen would have to endure sexual advances from gay men, upholding the false belief that gay men are predators with no control over their sexual desires. It is for these reasons that gays and lesbians must reject preconceived ideas and define themselves. By defining themselves, they gain the power to explore their individuality, take control of their lives, and eliminate stereotypes.

Things to Do

• Be vigilant about rejecting stereotypes and not surrendering your individuality.

• Those people who have incorporated stereotypes into their lives should realize that it is possible to change and redefine who they are.

• Begin redefining yourself by wiping the slate clean. By throwing out all stereotypical gay and lesbian traits, you will get closer to yourself. Now, from a distance, you can examine these traits thoroughly and, being true to yourself, determine if they really define who you are. Ask the question: am I comfortable with this appearance, behavior, and attitude? Some people will discover that they are, while others are not.

• Lipstick lesbians and macho gay men should also undergo this mental exercise, asking themselves if they are being true to their nature or just conforming to the backlash against stereotypes.

• Challenge gays and lesbians who seek approval from heterosexuals by incorporating stereotypes to the extent that they become caricatures. Inform them of the damage they are doing to themselves and others.

• Be careful not to stereotype other gays and lesbians.

• Make a list of all the stereotypes you can think of pertaining to gays and lesbians. Then for each item on the list identify a gay or lesbian person who doesn't fit the stereotype.

• Challenge heterosexuals who stereotype; inform them that gays and lesbians are as diverse in appearance, attitudes, and behavior as heterosexuals.

• Pursue careers that interest you, not what the stereotypers define as appropriate for gays and lesbians.

44
Accept Diversity in the Gay and Lesbian Community

BACKGROUND

When the gay and lesbian rights movement began in the early 1960s, its composition mirrored the power structure of American society in that it was primarily comprised of and controlled by mainstream European-American gays and lesbians. But over the course of time the multicultural nature of the community began to show as gays and lesbians from diverse ethnic, racial, class, religious, and national backgrounds formed their own organizations or joined the existing organizations and began contributing to the movement. This diversity is one of the strengths of the community, enriching it with energy and vitality and providing variation in regard to political affiliation, social ideas, religious customs, and cultural experiences.

Diversity, however, is a double-edged sword that can either enhance a community when its members are open-minded and accepting or can prompt fearful and insecure people into feeling prejudiced and behaving in a manner that is destructive to themselves and others. Although the gay and lesbian community in general has dealt well with its diversity, some tension exists between various groups. For example, a number of African-American lesbians have claimed that they feel unwelcome in certain bars and clubs. While it is to be expected that in a society with a history of racism some tension will linger between diverse groups, gays and lesbians from all groups must work hard to keep this tension to a minimum. To allow diversity to divide the movement would harm the struggle for civil rights and allow the antigay and lesbian forces to achieve their goals. By challenging prejudice immediately when it materializes, being sensitive to each other, respecting differences, and maintaining an inclusive attitude, the community will remain unified and strong.

Diversity within the gay and lesbian community is not limited to ethnicity, race, and class. Transgender and transsexual people contribute a great deal to the movement. The Stonewall Riot, which was a turning point in the struggle for gay and lesbian rights, was initiated by a group of transgender individuals. They had the courage to fight back when the police tried to arrest and humiliate them. The movement owes them a debt, and it is reprehensible that some mainstream-oriented gays and lesbians try to exclude them from the group. Keep in mind that gays and lesbians of all persuasions have two common enemies: homophobia and AIDS. And the movement needs all its members if it's going to defeat these enemies.

Things to Do

• Reach out to gays and lesbians from other groups and work together on projects and protest activity.

• There are hundreds of organizations that represent the different groups. To find the one you want, call the gay and lesbian community center or switchboard in your area.

• Gays and lesbians should not limit their membership and activity to the group that represents their social, racial, and ethnic background. They should also join national political organizations such as NGLTF and participate in the movement on this level.

RESOURCES

Below is a list of the main gay and lesbian multicultural and religious organizations. There are many others but it is impossible to list them all in this context.

Asians and Friends/New York
P.O. Box 3361
New York, NY 10163
718-488-0630

Black and White Men Together
2261 Market St., #506
San Francisco, CA 94114
415-826-BWMT

Gender Identity Alliance for Transsexuals
208 West 13th St,
New York, NY 10011
212-620-7310

Greater New York Gender Alliance (transgender)
330 West 45th St.
New York, NY 10036
212-765-3561

Irish Lesbian and Gay Organization (ILGO)
208 West 13th St.
New York, NY 10011
212-967-7711, ext. 3078

Men of All Colors Together/New York
P.O. Box 1518, Ansonia Station
New York, NY 10023
212-330-7678

National Coalition of Black Lesbians and Gays
505 8th Ave., 16th fl.
New York, NY 10018
212-563-8340

National Latino/A Lesbian and Gay Organization
703 G St. SE
Washington, DC 20003
202-544-0092

SAGE (Senior Action in a Gay Environment)
The Center
208 West 13th St.
New York, NY 10011
212-741-2247

South Asian Lesbian and Gay Association
170 East 3rd St.
New York, NY 10009
212-475-6486

Universal Fellowship of Metropolitan Churches
5300 Santa Monica Blvd., #304
Los Angeles, CA 90029
213-464-5100

World Congress of Gay and Lesbian Jewish Organizations
P.O. Box 3345
New York, NY 10008-3345

45
Support Gay and Lesbian Bookstores

BACKGROUND

Before the Stonewall Rebellion gays and lesbians had a difficult time finding books that dealt in a positive way with their experience. The main reason for this lack of material is not that gays and lesbians were not writing books, but that they were having difficulty finding publishers brave enough to meet their needs and explore this market. While underground publishing already existed, it was limited and mainly produced pulp fiction. In the 1970s a new generation of gay and lesbian writers decided that they were not going to wait around for publishers to get with it and began publishing their own books. Thus, with the emergence of houses such as Alyson, Naiad, Firebrand, and others, the gay and lesbian book publishing market was born.

Coinciding with the rise of this market came a proliferation of gay and lesbian bookstores. All large metropolitan areas have gay bookstores and they are a valuable resource for the community. They not only sell books from every genre, magazines, journals, videos, postcards, T-shirts, posters, and audio material, but many also sponsor events such as poetry readings, free movie viewing, book signings and provide space for bulletin boards, flyers, and free newspapers. Anyone looking for information about gay and lesbian events and organizations in their city can find this information in the bookstore. Whenever I travel to another city the first place I go to find out about the city's homosexual community is to the gay bookstore. Gay and lesbian bookstore owners and employees are involved in the community and can supply a wealth of information about the latest social and political trends. They also know their product and can recommend books to those customers who are confused by the large selection and uncertain about what to buy.

Although large, mainstream bookstores in metropolitan areas are now stocking gay and lesbian books, they cannot equal the role of the gay and lesbian bookstore as social center and meeting place.

Things to Do

• When possible, make a point of buying your books and magazines in gay and lesbian bookstores. They provide an important service for the community and deserve your support.

• Encourage your friends to support gay and lesbian bookstores.

• Remember the bookstores when it is time to buy gifts for friends and family members.

• If you work in any area of the publishing industry, join Publishing Triangle. (Their address and phone number is listed below.) This is a networking organization of gays and lesbians involved in publishing. They have regular meetings, print a newsletter, and sponsor an annual event called National Lesbian and Gay Book Month.

• If there is no gay or lesbian bookstore in your area, you

can order catalogs from the bookstores in large cities and shop by mail.

• Participate in events sponsored by the bookstores. You can meet authors, publishers, and even new friends.

RESOURCES

Publishing Triangle
P.O. Box 114
Prince St. Station
New York, NY 10012
212-572-6142

Bookstores

This is only a partial listing; there are many more. All bookstores listed below provide mail order service.

A Different Light
151 West 19th St.
New York, NY 10011
212-989-4850
fax: 212-989-2158
Mail-order number: 800-343-4002 (Canada too!)

489 Castro St.
San Francisco, CA 94114
415-431-0891

8853 Santa Monica Blvd.
West Hollywood, CA 90069
310-854-6601

Beyond the Closet Bookstore
1501 Belmont Ave.
Seattle, WA 98122
206-322-4609

Glad Day Bookshop
673 Boylston St., 2nd fl.
Boston, MA 02116
617-267-3010

Judith's Room (books for women, closed Monday)
681 Washington St.
New York, NY 10014
212-727-7330

Lambda Rising
1625 Connecticut Ave. NW
Washington, DC 20009
202-462-6969

Oscar Wilde Memorial Bookshop (world's first gay and lesbian bookstore—founded 1967)
15 Christopher St.
New York, NY 10014
212-255-8097

People Like Us Books
3321 N. Clark St.
Chicago, IL 60657
312-248-6363

46
Ask Librarians to Stock Gay and Lesbian Books

BACKGROUND

There are different kinds of libraries. College and university libraries cater to the academic needs of faculty and students and they provide necessary research material such as periodicals, journals, dictionaries, textbooks, nonfiction geared toward academic disciplines, and classic fiction and poetry. A good academic library, whether or not the college offers gay and lesbian studies, will stock *The Journal of Homosexuality* and other gay- and lesbian-themed material in the social studies section. Since most large universities now have a gay and lesbian studies department, the students, faculty, administrators, and alumni/ae have access to an abundance of material dealing with gay and lesbian issues. The general public, however, does not have access to college libraries and must rely on public libraries to borrow books and other material. With the exception of the main branches in large cities, public libraries tend to be deficient when it comes to gay and lesbian books and magazines. Censorship is the main reason for this deficiency. Libraries are constantly under pressure from self-righteous community groups to deny the public access to material they consider to be offensive. As a result, public libraries have become one of the battlegrounds in the struggle for gay and lesbian rights.

Public libraries are funded mainly by the taxpayers and they therefore have a moral and ethical obligation to cater to the needs of all taxpayers in the community. As taxpaying citizens, gays and lesbians are deprived of the right to reap the benefits of their hard-earned money. With regard to certain public institutions such as libraries and schools their taxes support the needs of the heterosexual majority while they have to settle for less or nothing. It's time for gays, lesbians, and their supporters to start putting pressure on these institutions and demand the services they pay for.

Generally it is not the librarians themselves who censor gay and lesbian books. Their job is to keep their libraries well stocked and up to date, and for them to support and enforce censorship would be counterproductive. Librarians are forced to remove books from the shelves or to keep them locked up in areas of the library that are off-limits to young people. Unless gays and lesbians speak up and counter the pressure from the homophobic groups, librarians will receive no support in their efforts to provide for the entire community.

You should know book burning is not a thing of the past. On September 15, 1994 a book burning took place on the grounds of the Kansas Public Library. Many gay-and-lesbian-themed books were included in the burning.

Things to Do

• Support the American Library Association Gay and Lesbian Task Force.

• Become a member of the Freedom to Read Foundation.

Founded by the American Library Association, this organization fights book censorship on every level. As a member, you will receive its quarterly newsletter.

• Discuss the censorship of gay and lesbian books with the local public librarian.

• Make suggestions to the librarian about which gay and lesbian books and magazines you would like the library to stock. For example, every library in the country should subscribe to *The Advocate*.

• Local gay and lesbian organizations and individuals should constantly pressure the public libraries.

• If their requests go unheeded, then they must complain to politicians and local officials.

• Donate your used (in good condition) gay and lesbian books to your local library.

• If you suspect that the librarian is the censor, report him or her to the Freedom to Read Foundation.

• If you have access to a college library, take advantage of its gay and lesbian resources.

• If you find your college library to be lacking in gay and lesbian material, complain to the librarian and the academic dean.

RESOURCES

American Library Association
Freedom to Read Foundation
50 East Huron St.
Chicago, IL 60611
312-944-6780

American Library Association
Gay and Lesbian Task Force
(same address)

47
Be Visible: Don't Be Afraid to Display the Symbols

For this once hidden minority, widespread visibility is the absolute condition for all progress.

—TORIE OSBORN

BACKGROUND

People use symbols as a way of demonstrating unity within a group or to bring attention to causes. In the past gays and lesbians used symbols, known only to the group, as a means of communication to inform each other without stating it openly (which could have been dangerous) that they were "in the life." Fortunately, today gays and lesbians do not have to rely on such cryptic measures to meet others, but symbols still play an important role. In 1993, I made my first trip to Provincetown, which is a predominantly gay town on Cape Cod, and I remember feeling great satisfaction, solidarity, and pride when I saw the rainbow flag displayed throughout the town. Symbols help generate visibility and represent unity in the struggle for gay and lesbian civil rights. Some people prefer not to display symbols, but others feel comfortable displaying symbols that represent their beliefs, affiliations, and commitments. For those who want to add to their visibility there are a variety of items available such as buttons and pins, flags, hats, posters, T-shirts, jewelry, and bumper stickers. You can buy these products in most gay and lesbian bookstores or you can order them through the mail from the gay-owned businesses listed below.

SYMBOLS

Rainbow flag: The flag represents unity and has become the dominant symbol for gay and lesbian liberation. Many people find it more appealing than the pink triangle because of its positive connotations.

Pink triangle: Gay men in Nazi concentration camps were forced to wear the pink triangle with one point downward to indicate inversion. Activists reclaimed the symbol to bring attention to gay oppression.

Black triangle: Lesbians in Nazi concentration camps were forced to wear this symbol.

Freedom rings: Six rings with the rainbow colors and usually worn on a chain.

Merged gender symbols: The universal gender symbols, two circles each with an arrow for gay men and two circles each with a cross for lesbians.

Lambda: This Greek letter symbolizes the reconciliation of opposites and change. It is used by both gay men and lesbians.

Labrys: The amazon ax represents female strength and has become a symbol of lesbianism.

The red ribbon for AIDS awareness: Although the red ribbon is not associated with homosexuality or lesbianism, many people, including heterosexuals, concerned about AIDS like to wear it.

RESOURCES

Proud Enterprises
496A Hudson St.
New York, NY 10014
800-47-PROUD
fax: 212-691-3448

Shocking Gray
1216 East Euclid
San Antonio, TX 78212-4159
800-788-4729
fax: 210-224-1043

48
Support Gay and Lesbian Cultural Events

*The artwork we choose to fund is not funded based on
content. What we fund is based on artistic merit. And that
can come from anyone, gay or straight.*

*—Jane Alexander, Chairwoman of the
National Endowment of the Arts*

BACKGROUND

Gay and lesbian artists have always depicted their experience,
but, as usual, homosexual material was censored from the mainstream culture and these artists were denied access to resources
such as performance spaces, galleries, movie and television stu-
dios, and funding. In order to have their work produced many
conformed to the rules established by a homophobic society in-
tent on keeping portrayals of the gay and lesbian experience out
of the dominant culture. For example, they would transform
their representation of a gay or lesbian romance into a heterosexual romance. In 1936, when MGM bought the rights to the
movie production of Lillian Hellman's play *The Children's Hour*,
they forced her to rewrite the script and delete all references to
lesbianism. Hellman wanted the movie produced and cooper-
ated. She changed the lesbian character into a heterosexual and
the central plot into an adulterous heterosexual affair. Some gay
and lesbian artists worked for the movie and theater industries as
actors, screen- and scriptwriters, directors, and set designers.
They used their creative energy to depict the heterosexual expe-

rience. This in itself would not have been a negative thing had they also been allowed to depict honestly their own experiences as gays and lesbians.

In recent years gays and lesbian artists have become assertive and unwilling to compromise their art to promote heterosexism. As a result, there is now a vibrant cultural scene that gays and lesbians can relate to. This art scene includes, but is not limited to, film, theater, and music, and some of the artwork finds its way into the mainstream. Some gay-themed plays such as *Angels in America* appeal to all audiences, gays and heterosexuals included. But the cultural scene within the community includes works and events that appeal mainly to gays and lesbians. Performing arts, cabarets, music and film festivals, art exhibitions, and the Gay Games, a sporting event, are financed by gays and lesbians and aimed at their community. Heterosexuals, if they are interested, are welcome to participate in most of these events. But without predominant gay and lesbian support this cultural scene cannot survive.

Things to Do

- Keep up to date with the cultural scene. Gay magazines and newspapers have extensive coverage of this scene.
- Make a commitment to attend plays, art exhibitions, and poetry readings on a regular basis and encourage your friends to do the same. (It's also a great way to meet people with similar interests.)
- Give financial support to organizations that sponsor these events.
- Write to the NEA and express your support for its inclusive policies toward gays and lesbians and gratitude for its unwillingness to cave into pressure from the antigay and lesbian politicians and the religious right.
- If you are an artist, apply to the NEA for a grant.

RESOURCES

Gay Cable Network (produces *Party Talk* and other cable programs)
150 West 26th St.
New York, NY 10001
212-727-8850
fax: 212-229-2347

Dyke TV
P.O. Box 55, Prince St. Station
New York, NY 10002
212-343-9335
fax: 212-343-9337

Leslie-Lohman Gay Art Foundation
127 Prince St.
New York, NY 10012
212-673-7007

Lesbian and Gay Chorus
P.O. Box 65285
Washington, DC 20035
202-546-1549

Lesbian and Gay Film Festival
1229 W. Belmont
Chicago, IL 60657
312-281-8788

Lesbian and Gay Film Festival
462 Broadway #510
New York, NY 10013
212-966-5656

Michigan Womyn's Music Festival
P.O. Box 22
Walhalla, MI 49458
616-757-4766

National Endowment for the Arts
1100 Pennsylvania Ave. NW
Washington, DC 20506
202-682-5400

New York City Gay Men's Chorus
P.O. Box 587, Murray Hill Station
New York, NY 10156
212-924-7770

Persona Video
P.O. Box 14022
San Francisco, CA 94114
415-775-6143

49
Write About Your Efforts and Results

How to Make the World a Better Place for Gays and Lesbians provides you with many suggestions on what you can do as an individual to help the cause of gay and lesbian rights. The actions you take, no matter how small, will produce a result. The result can range from bringing someone's attention to an injustice to a direct action by a person in power to eliminate the injustice. Whatever the effort and result is, it is important for you to keep a concrete record of your actions. This will provide you with evidence and give you satisfaction when you see on paper an outcome that can only be positive. The writing process is an intense, deep, thinking process. And once you start writing about a subject ideas emerge. When your subject is how to fight homophobia you may develop new ideas, and your own list of things to do for the advancement of gay and lesbian rights.

Things to Do

• Make a commitment to do something every day to fight homophobia. If you are a busy person and cannot become involved on a daily basis, then determine how much time and resources you can afford to devote to the cause and stick with your commitment.

• Keep a separate journal specifically for recording your efforts and results. Be sure to include what prompted you to take the action, the date, what the action was, to whom it was directed, and the results.

• Keep a separate file of your correspondence in regard to the actions you take. Also, save copies of your letters, faxes, and postcards and list all phone calls you make and receive, whom you spoke with, their position, what they said, and what they said they would do.

• If you get no immediate results, then repeat the action, follow up, and become a nuisance until you get a response. Don't be afraid to annoy people. Agitation is necessary for change to occur.

• Share your information and results with gay and lesbian activists.

50
Share This Book
with Others

Now that you have read this book, not only will you take action, but you will begin to talk more about homophobia and what can be done to eliminate it from society. People you know will notice this commitment and concern. They will see that you have made a difference and realize that they too can contribute to this important struggle and ask you questions about what can be done.

In order to secure gay and lesbian rights everyone needs to become involved. You can encourage people to join in and provide the resources they need by passing on this book to friends, relatives, and others or by sharing the information it contains.

Stay proud, optimistic, and dedicated to the cause and, above all, take action!

About the Author

Una Fahy was born in Ireland and immigrated to the United States in 1973. In the late 1970s she confronted and accepted her lesbianism. From that point on she became involved in the gay and lesbian rights movement. Ms. Fahy graduated from Marymount Manhattan College with a degree in English literature. Currently, Una lives and works in New York City. She is a member of the Gay and Lesbian Alliance Against Defamation (GLAAD).